Map: Zululand & KwaZulu-Natal Coast

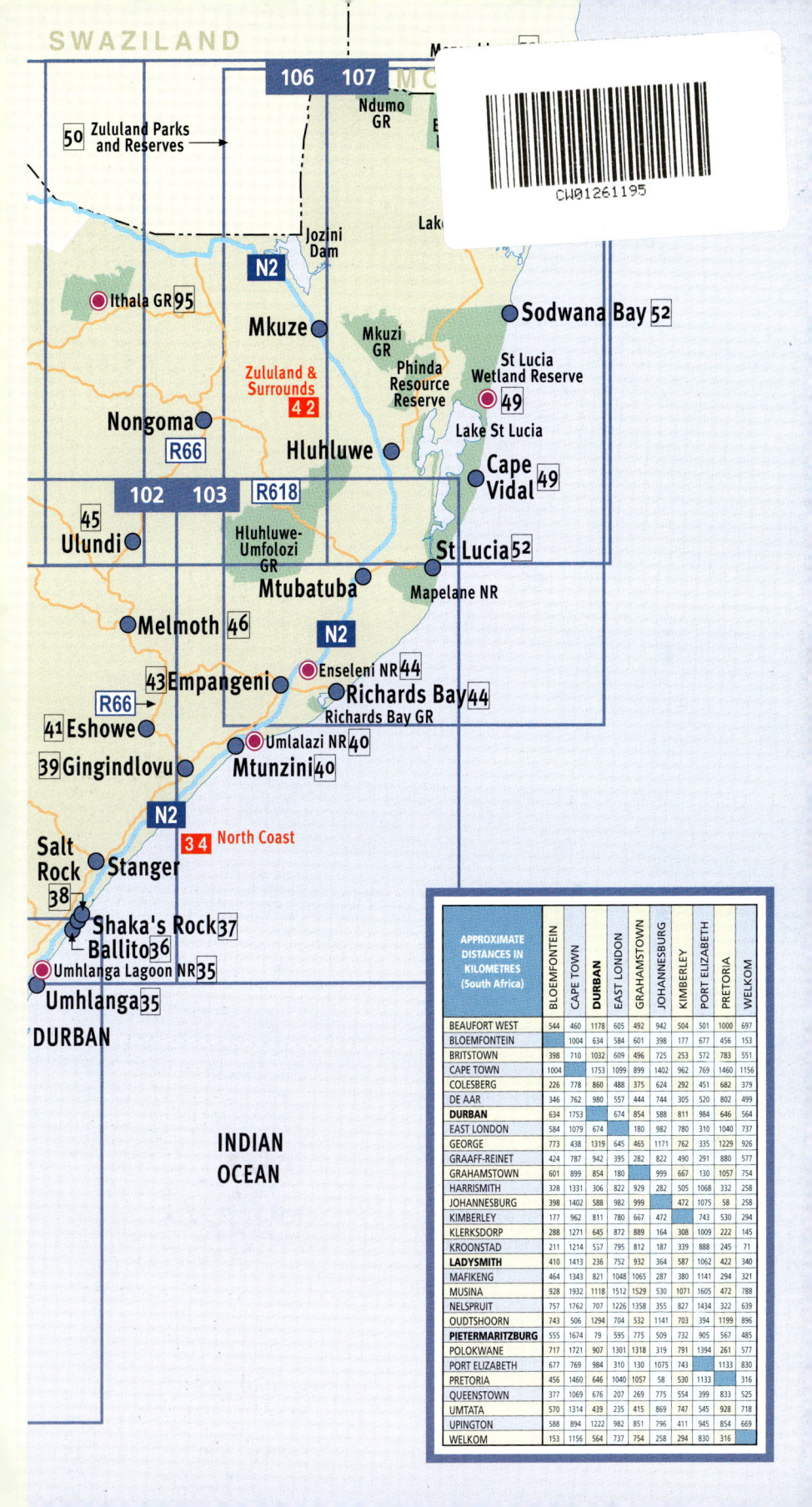

SWAZILAND

- Ithala GR 95
- Nongoma
- Mkuze
- Hluhluwe
- Sodwana Bay 52
- St Lucia Wetland Reserve 49
- Cape Vidal 49
- Ulundi 45
- Mtubatuba
- St Lucia 52
- Mapelane NR
- Melmoth 46
- Empangeni 43
- Enseleni NR 44
- Richards Bay 44
- Richards Bay GR
- Eshowe 41
- Gingindlovu 39
- Umlalazi NR 40
- Mtunzini 40
- North Coast 34
- Salt Rock 38
- Stanger
- Shaka's Rock 37
- Ballito 36
- Umhlanga Lagoon NR 35
- Umhlanga 35
- DURBAN

Zululand Parks and Reserves 50
Zululand & Surrounds 42
Ndumo GR
Jozini Dam
Mkuzi GR
Phinda Resource Reserve
Lake St Lucia
Hluhluwe-Umfolozi GR

N2, R66, R618, 102, 103, 106, 107

INDIAN OCEAN

APPROXIMATE DISTANCES IN KILOMETRES (South Africa)

	BLOEMFONTEIN	CAPE TOWN	DURBAN	EAST LONDON	GRAHAMSTOWN	JOHANNESBURG	KIMBERLEY	PORT ELIZABETH	PRETORIA	WELKOM
BEAUFORT WEST	544	460	1178	605	492	942	504	501	1000	697
BLOEMFONTEIN		1004	634	584	601	398	177	677	456	153
BRITSTOWN	398	710	1032	609	496	725	253	572	783	551
CAPE TOWN	1004		1753	1099	899	1402	962	769	1460	1156
COLESBERG	226	778	860	488	375	624	292	451	682	379
DE AAR	346	762	980	557	444	744	305	520	802	499
DURBAN	634	1753		674	854	588	811	984	646	564
EAST LONDON	584	1079	674		180	982	780	310	1049	737
GEORGE	773	438	1319	645	465	1171	762	335	1229	926
GRAAFF-REINET	424	787	942	395	282	822	490	291	880	577
GRAHAMSTOWN	601	899	854	180		999	667	130	1057	754
HARRISMITH	328	1331	306	822	929	282	505	1068	332	258
JOHANNESBURG	398	1402	588	982	999		472	1075	58	258
KIMBERLEY	177	962	811	780	667	472		743	530	294
KLERKSDORP	288	1271	645	872	889	164	308	1009	222	145
KROONSTAD	211	1214	557	795	812	187	339	888	245	71
LADYSMITH	410	1413	236	752	932	364	587	1062	422	340
MAFIKENG	464	1343	821	1048	1065	287	380	1141	294	321
MUSINA	928	1932	1118	1512	1529	530	1071	1605	472	788
NELSPRUIT	757	1762	707	1226	1358	355	827	1434	322	639
OUDTSHOORN	743	506	1294	704	532	1141	703	394	1199	896
PIETERMARITZBURG	555	1674	79	595	775	509	732	905	567	485
POLOKWANE	717	1721	907	1301	1318	319	791	1394	261	577
PORT ELIZABETH	677	769	984	310	130	1075	743		1133	830
PRETORIA	456	1460	646	1040	1057	58	530	1133		316
QUEENSTOWN	377	1069	676	207	269	775	554	399	833	525
UMTATA	570	1314	439	235	415	869	747	545	928	718
UPINGTON	588	894	1222	982	851	796	411	945	854	669
WELKOM	153	1156	564	737	754	258	294	830	316	

MapStudio

First edition published in 2004 by Map Studio

www.mapstudio.co.za
0860 10 50 50

HEAD OFFICE
Cornelis Struik House
80 McKenzie Street
Cape Town
Tel: 021 462 4360

PO Box 1144
Cape Town, 8000

SALES OFFICES
Map Studio Johannesburg
7 Wessel Road, Rivonia
Tel: 011 807 2292

Map Studio Cape Town
Unit 7, M5 Freeway Park
Maitland
Tel: 021 510 4311

Map Studio Durban
Shop 3A, 47 Intersite Avenue
Umgeni Park
Tel: 031 263 1203

ISBN: 1 86809 742 0
10 9 8 7 6 5 4 3 2 1

Printed in Singapore by
Tien Wah Press (Pte) Ltd.

Copyright © 2004 in text: Map Studio
Copyright © 2004 in maps: Map Studio
Copyright © 2004 in photographs:
Photographers as credited (below)
Copyright © 2004 Map Studio

Photographic Credits
t = top, c = centre, b = bottom, l = left, r = right
Ithala Development Finance Corporation 25.
Durban International Convention Centre 21, 24.
Struik Image Library
Colour Library 4, 16t, 35. **Keith Young** 28, 37, 50c, 72t.
Ariadne van Zandbergen 50t, 75.
Lanz von Horsten 34, 44, 54b. **Leonard Hoffmann** 52.
Nigel J Dennis 47c, 57, 90, 93. **Peter Pickford** 30, 31, 47t, 53. **Rod Haestier** 10t&b, 60, 63.
Roger de la Harpe 3, 8t, 9tl&b, 10c, 11c, 41, 43, 45, 46, 48b, 65, 67-70, 74, 77, 86. **Shaen Adey** 8c, 9t, 11t&b, 14, 17, 20, 23, 26-27, 39, 47b, 48t&c, 50b, 59, 64, 66b, 71, 72b, 78-79, 80b, 82, 91, 95-96. **Walter Knirr** 17b, 22, 54t, 80t&c, 84, 86t.
Cover: Zulu beadwork.
Page 3: Zulu beadwork.
Page 4: Kosi Bay.
Page 14: Durban city hall.
Page 54: Drakensberg.

All rights reserved. No part of this publication may be reproduced, stored in a retrieval system or transmitted, in any form or by any means, electronic, mechanical, photocopying, recording or otherwise, without the permission of the publishers and copyright holders.

Although every effort has been made to ensure that this guide is up to date and current at time of going to print, the Publisher accepts no responsibility or liability for any loss, injury or inconvenience incurred by readers or travellers using this guide.

Map Studio Tourist team
Dénielle Lategan
Edward Hill
Elaine Fick
John Loubser
Lois O'Brien
Mark Hedington
Maryna Beukes
Myrna Collins
Ryan Africa
Simon Lewis
Broderick Kupka (Sales: Johannesburg)
Gina Moniz (Sales: Cape Town / Durban)

Special thanks to Leizel Brown and Cliff Linton-Walls for their contributions.

Been there, done that?
Please let us know if you find any interesting information on your travels through KwaZulu-Natal or notice any changes. We'll reward the best contributions with a copy of this guide when we update.

Send your contributions to:
Simon Lewis
Map Studio Tourist
PO Box 1144
Cape Town 8000

or e-mail tourist@mapstudio.co.za

KWAZULU-NATAL

KwaZulu-Natal KwaZulu-Natal K

Zulu-Natal **KwaZulu-Natal** KwaZu

Known as the Last Outpost of the British Empire, Natal's history and tradition is littered with colonial influences and interference.

Introduction Introduction Introdu

If you're into consistency, then you're into the Durban lifestyle and climate. As long as you like your weather conditions to be of the subtropical variety then you'll be in tourist heaven, as the seasons flow in an uninterrupted cycle of temperature and rainfall patterns. It rains a lot, but you won't worry about being flooded. It can get real hot and humid at times (especially in summer), but rather be hot in sandals and shorts than cold in jersey and boots! There's loads more to do besides enjoying the countless splendid beaches running along the coast, but if the beach isn't your scene then you're really missing out, especially as the warm Indian Ocean water is great for swimming in all year round. Durban is a holidaymaker's paradise, with the Golden Mile of luxury hotels lining the beachfront, while the Midlands Meander through English-like countryside (serviced by gorgeous country houses) provides a totally different diversion, laced with arts and crafts outlets. An historical blot on the landscape, the Battlefields Route is a sad – yet popular! – reminder of much bloodshed and violence in the area ... and naturally the Drakensberg mountain range and the Greater St Lucia Wetland Park are two massive tourist magnets.

FIVE FAMOUS COASTS
The Hibiscus Coast
The Wild Coast
The Dolphin Coast
The Elephant Coast
The Sugar Coast

- 42 Tourist region maps
- 42 Chapter opener maps
- ● Point of interest

FIVE TOP TRIPS
The vintage steam train the Banana Express.
A Ricksha ride down Durban's Golden Mile.
Brave Oribi Gorge's foofy slide.
Cruise along the Midlands Meander.
Hang Ten on one of thousands of waves along the coastline.

FIVE THINGS ANYONE CAN DO
Take in the majesty of the Temple of Understanding.
Step back in time at Shakaland.
Enjoy the sight of exotic subtropical birds.
Enjoy a delicious bunny chow.
Buy traditional Zulu beadwork or statues as a memento of your visit.

The mighty Zulu nation was made up of fierce and proud warriors who controlled the region, as well as creative artists and craftspeople.

Introduction Introduction Intro

Durban Maps
- 18-19 — Durban CBD
- 20 — Walking Durban
- 21 — International Convention Centre
- 22 — Durban Botanic Gardens
- 23 — uShaka Marine World
- 25 — Durban Nightlife
- 26 — Umgeni River Bird Park
  — Beachwood Mangrove Swamp
- 27 — Inanda Trail
- 28-29 — Greater Durban
- 30 — Kenneth Stainbank NR
  — Krantzkloof NR
  — Bluff NR
- 31 — Greater Durban Reserves and Parks

FIVE FOR THE RELIC HUNTER
Dick King statue in Durban.
Gandhi Memorial in Pietermaritzburg.
The Battlefields Route.
Shaka's Rock, Shaka's tree, Coward's Bush ...
The recent Iron Age discoveries at Salt Rock.

7

Durban began life as Port Natal, a cutoff trading post for traders on the high seas and a refuge for the great white hunters.

Historical Historical Historical Hi

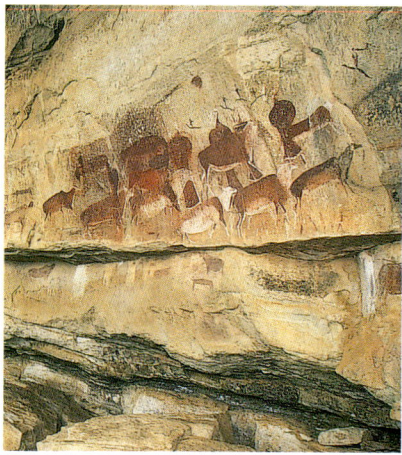

Top: An open-air museum depicting the life of the San people.
Above: Rock art found in the Kamberg.

CASTAWAY
Tourists today can understand the pulling power of Durban's glorious seafront and coastline: it's magical and magnificent. In fact, Durban's seafront has had a magnetic effect on people for centuries. The Stone Age San hunter-gatherers apparently enjoyed Durban's warmer winters compared with the icy conditions they were used to up in the mountains. During the Iron Age migrants from Central Africa shifted their focus to 'Durbs', followed centuries later by swashbuckling pirates and, oddly enough, shipwrecked European explorers who were literally forced to drop anchor and setup home here. As with any valuable real estate, there's been a whole lot of movement around Durbs.

SHAKA ZULU
Surely South Africa's greatest historical icon, Shaka, king of the Zulu nation, remains shrouded in myth and fable, has been portrayed on TV by a soccer goalkeeper, and his name is borne by streets, trees, rocks, guest houses, lodges, and so on (if only he had registered his name when he had the chance!). One of Shaka's major strengths was his military ability, and he adopted a system of enlisting into his forces prisoners of war from previous victories, thus adding to his might. He was a tough taskmaster and something of a perfectionist, and it's said that his soldiers had to remain celibate during their time in Shaka's 'armed forces'. The penalty for breaking that rule was DEATH ... the same penalty employed on anyone who displayed any fear. Another innovation was moving from the previous 'throw, turn and run' tactic of warrior attack by developing the short-handled assegai, thus forcing his warriors into close combat that broke down the opponents' defence. In addition, he was a master of creating ingenious military formations to baffle the enemy. His legacy is that of unifying many of southern Africa's tribes as well as staving off European advances, yet his death (aged 42) came at the hands of his half-brothers – stabbed to death, his body was left for the vultures.

Vasco da Gama called out 'land-ho' on Christmas Day, 1497 ... and named the coastline he saw in front of him 'Natal'.

Historical Historical Historical Historical

Above: *Memorial to the battle at Spioenkop.*
Right: *Zulu warriors in traditional dress.*

RESISTANCE IS NOT FUTILE
One of the world's greatest-ever statesmen and leaders, Mahatma Gandhi spent many years living and working in KwaZulu-Natal. A statue commemorates the fateful day in 1893 when he tried to buy a first-class train ticket to Jo'burg, but was denied because of the country's race laws. There are many statues and memorials to this great man throughout the province in which his acclaimed passive resistance movement (aka satyagraha) first saw the light of day. A lawyer, Gandhi came to South Africa to assist fellow Indians in their plight – they had been brought over in their thousands as indentured plantation hands to build the region's economy. The Indian population have since taken their place in Durban society, carved their niche and made their mark on the province, adding a rich cultural legacy to a region awash with cultures, histories and religions. Gandhi's varied and selfless CV includes carrying stretchers during the Anglo-Boer War: truly a man of the people!

THE GREATEST RIDE IN TOWN
One of the country's great local icons, Dick King has his own fair share of memorials throughout South Africa. Back in 1842 (before cellphones or normal phones!) King saddled up and covered almost 1000km from Durban to Grahamstown to raise the alarm to the British that their troops were besieged by the Boers. King was aided in his epic journey by a 16-year-old tracker, Ndongeni. Even earlier (in 1827!) a 15-year-old sailor lead an expedition on foot for three weeks on a 960km round trip from Durban to Delagoa Bay to pick up vital medical supplies. His name has gone down in history as John Ross ... not his real name, as he made it up when he ran away to sea as a 12-year-old! And you think you had it tough growing up!

Boer War memorabilia from the Voortrekker museum in Pietermaritzburg.

The mighty Tugela River is ready to offer up what you want: a hard-as-nails ride or a dreamy drift downstream. Either way, rafting the river is unforgettable.

Activities Activities Activities Ac

You can enjoy a gentle stroll for a few hours, take a morning to hike around areas such as Cobham, Bushman's Nek, Garden Castle and Loteni, maybe see some San rock art, mountain pools, waterfalls and streams, or enjoy hilltop views that don't demand a mule and a sherpa to reach. You can take your pick of some of these activities and still be back at your hotel or B&B in time for lunch! The more experienced and dedicated can hike all day to explore deeper into the region's foothills and valleys. Naturally you can extend your escapade to an overnight excursion, stretching your hike for as long as you can manage. A popular overnight trip is the five-day Giant's Cup Trail in the Southern Drakensberg, with huts for hikers to sleep in. The Giant's Cup Trail starts on the Sani Pass road and finishes at Bushman's Nek, but there is the option of doing individual sections if you don't have the time or endurance for the five-day affair. Overnighting can also be done in one of the many mountain caves or by pitching your tent where you decide to stop (be environmentally aware and don't camp on the bank of a stream or in caves adorned with bushman paintings). For the rugged hiker and climber there are 26 peaks that top the 10,000-feet (3,050m) mark in the Southern Drakensberg, with Hodgson's Peak, The Rhino and Thabana Ntlenyana among the favourites.

LIFE'S A BEACH
Enjoy nature at its most enticing with a choice of stupendous beaches running up and down the coast, all brimming with fish and waves to catch. Families are well catered for with a string of tidal pools and other facilities to please those less pumped up on adrenaline. Durban and KZN is all about the beach ... and its soft sand, tropical climate and comfortable weather (a far cry from the guts needed for swimming at one of Clifton's beaches in Cape Town).

Top: *Surfing, what KZN is known best for!*
Above: *The annual Dusi canoe marathon.*
Below: *Sardine Run activity along the coast.*

TAKE A HIKE
Hiking is one of the Drakensberg's most common and popular pursuits, offering opportunities for all levels and schedules.

Be daring and see the majesty of the Dolphin Coast from a different angle ... take a scenic microlight flight and smile for the birdies!

Activities Activities Activities Activiti

Above: Hiking with a guide in the Umfolozi Game Reserve.
Below: Hanggliders near Howick.
Bottom: Get high and take a balloon ride for fabulous views.

A SHOAL THING, CHINA
Scuba divers and snorkellers will be loving their time spent on this coast with its multitude of great diving spots. The famed Aliwal Shoal was rated one of the world's Top 10 dive sites by the even more illustrious step-nephew of Neptune, French diving legend Jacques Cousteau. The shoal is the jewel of the south coast's already glittering crown and is filthy rich in marine and plant life, while offering really good visibility for divers. The Shoal lies treacherously close to the shoreline and is close on a kilometer wide in places – not surprisingly, it has claimed its fair share of ships in its time. Lander's Reef off Scottburgh beach is another magnificent spot for those keen on deep breaths and lots of bubbles bursting up above their heads. At times reaching depths as great as 36m, the reef is awash with plantlife and reef fish (enhanced by visibility in the region of 15m), as well as some exciting shipwrecks that lie in wait (be sure to follow usual shipwreck procedures and policies!).

CAST AWAY
The warm Agulhas current that flows south brings with it a treasure trove of fish species to entice anglers and fishermen, as well as enthusiasts of the annual Sardine Run, which sees millions of sardines migrating along the coast ... dragging in tow with them a good array of marine predators. Plenty to catch out at sea, on the countless piles of rocks that jut into the ocean all along the coast ... and even from the beach itself. If you're a fisherman you'll be pretty damn angry if you spend time in KZN without your trusty rod and lucky hat!
And lets not even mention all the trout over in 'them thar hills' ...

Durban is well served by a generally reliable transport infrastructure – trains run fairly regularly from the city to the beach resorts.

Getting There

The Banana Express (inset)

Port Shepstone
- SOUTH WHARF
  - Boat cruise on Umzimkulu River
Izotsha
- HISTORIC LIGHTHOUSE
- NYAMAZANE GAME RANCH
  - Bushveld cuisine
  - Game drive
- IZOTSHA : AYTON MANOR
  - Zakhele Hand Creations
  - Ayton Manor House
  - Tranquil Garden
  - Swimming
  - Quad biking
Paddock
- PADDOCK STATION
  - BBQ lunch or picnic
  - Visit museum in old stationmaster's house
- ZULU CHIEFTANS COUNTRYSIDE

OR

- IZOTSHA : SNAKE PARK
  - Pure Venom Reptile Farm
- VULINDLELA TOURS
  - African themed tour
  - African cuisine
  - Sites
  - Nyandezulu falls
  - Gamalakhe township
  - Umzumbe river valley
- ORIBI GORGE : HOTEL
  - Lunch at hotel
  - Viewpoint of Gorge
  - Adventure options
    - Abseiling
    - Wild Swings
    - River Rafting

Map locations

SWAZILAND

Paulpietersburg, Itala NR, Louwsburg, Newcastle, Utrecht, Vryheid, Chelmsford Nature Reserve, Glencoe, Dundee, Ulundi, Van Reenen, Mont-aux Sources, Royal Natal National Park, Ladysmith, Colenso, Melmoth, Bergville, Cathedral Peak, Weenen GR, Weenen, Nkwalini, Cathkin Peak, Drakensberg Sun, Champagne Castle, Ntabamhlope, Estcourt, Greytown, Kranskop, Gingindlovu, Giant's Castle, Natal Drakensberg Park, Loteni, Nottingham Road, Mooi River, Darnall, Stanger, Shaka's Rock, Salt Rock, Ballito, Vergelegen, Howick, PIETERMARITZBURG, Tongaat, Sani Pass, KwaMashu, Umhlanga, Underberg, Pinetown, DURBAN, Drakensberg Gardens, Umlazi, Isipingo, Umbogintwini, Matatiele, Ixopo, Kingsburgh, Amanzimtoti, Vernon Crookes NR, Umkomaas, Sezela, Scottburgh, Park Rynie, Kokstad, Harding, Hibberdene, Stafford's Post, Oribi Gorge NR, Marburg, Umtentweni, Port Shepstone, Paddock, Izotsha, Uvongo, Umtamvuna NR, Margate, Ramsgate, Southbroom, Port Edward

LESOTHO

12

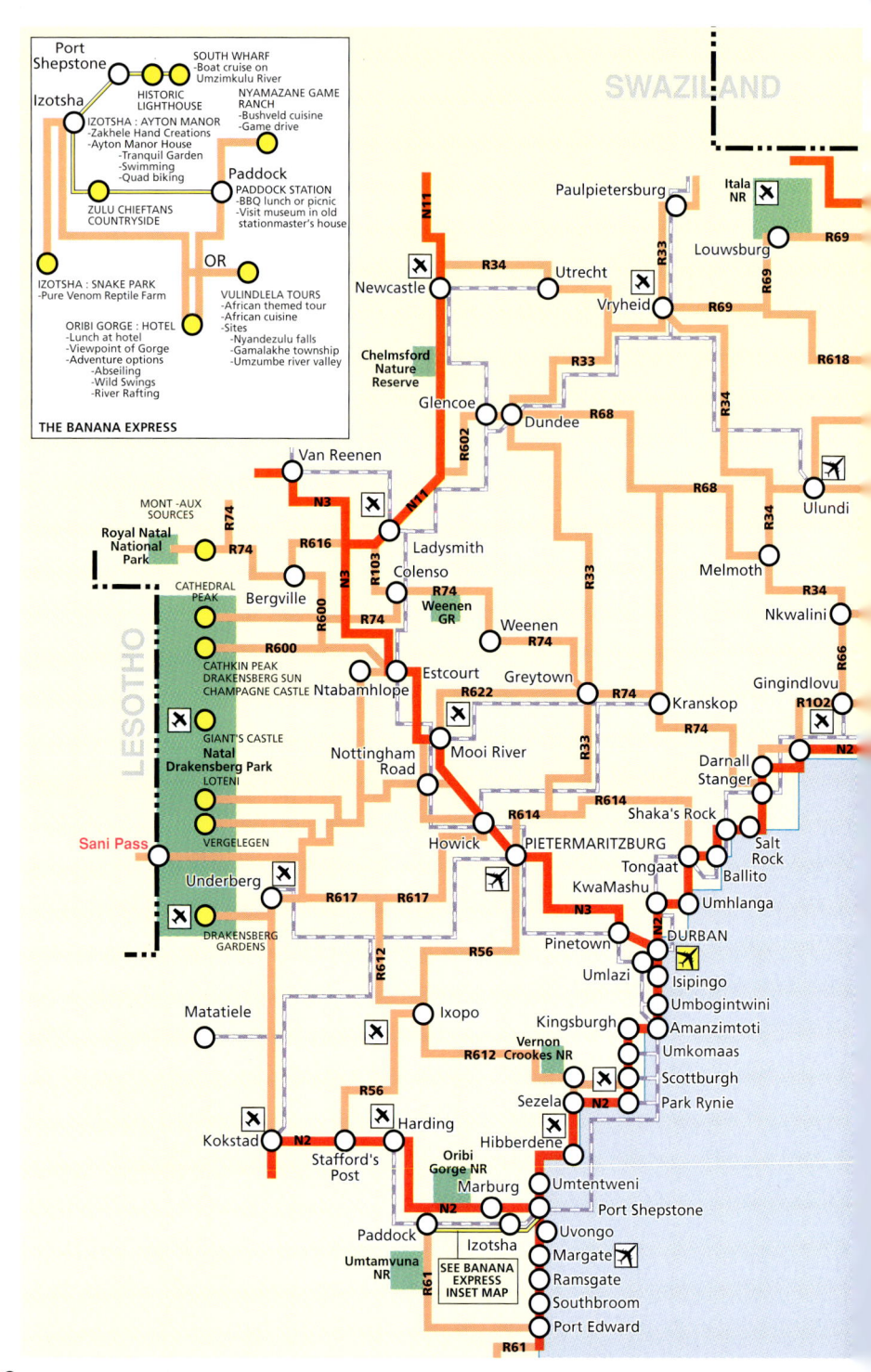

A vintage steam train with mass appeal, the Banana Express is a step back in time to relaxed travel with an eye on the window rather than on the clock.

Getting There

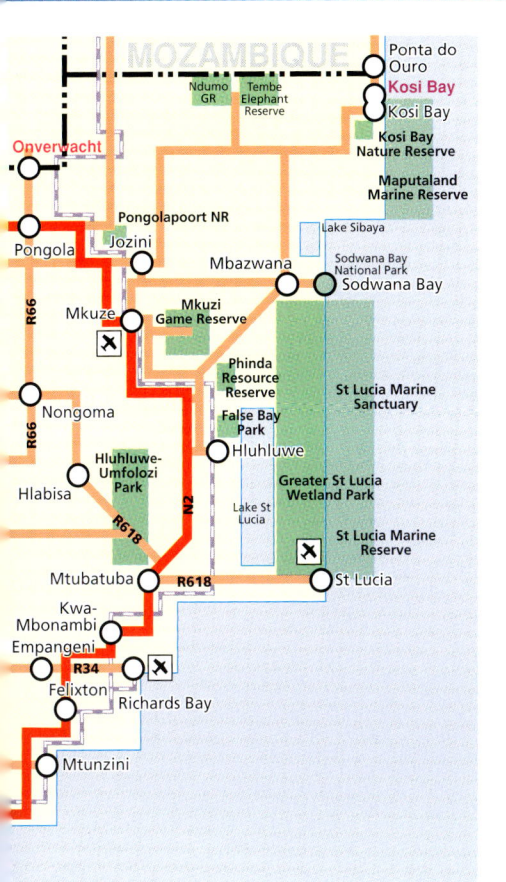

Durban International Airport is not recognised as an international airport to the same extent as Cape Town and Johannesburg. However, due to a good percentage of international flights stopping en route to overseas destinations, it has excellent facilities to manage the large numbers of visitors from overseas as well as South Africans travelling internally to and from Durban. Domestic flights are available to all major centres on regular and well-planned schedules that satisfy both international and local travellers. Once travellers have landed at Durban International they are able to use regular bus services for the short journey to the central business district and the city centre. Airport facilities for domestic travel are also available on the south coast at Margate and further north, serving the busy Richard's Bay area. Tourists and visitors can move around on the wide network of bus routes throughout the city, although this is not recommended at night. Sedan taxis offer an alternative and convenient form of transport around the city.

Steam train enthusiasts will enjoy the Banana Express. This narrow-gauge steam train leaves Port Shepstone every Thursday puffing along the coast and then winding through banana and sugar plantations on its inland journey to the village of Izotsha, before returning to the coast. Even more interesting is the Wednesday Banana Express trip from Port Shepstone to Paddock, a distance of some 39km and climbing to a height of 550m. Visitors are then taken on a guided walk in the Oribi Gorge Nature Reserve where they enjoy a traditional South African braai or barbeque before boarding the train once again to return to Port Shepstone.

Legend:
- NATIONAL HIGHWAY
- ALL OTHER ROADS
- Ballito ○ CITY & TOWN
- Kosi Bay ○ BORDER POST
- HOTEL OR LODGE
- INTERNATIONAL AIRPORT
- OTHER AIRPORT / AIRFIELD
- R37 ROUTE NUMBER
- INTERNATIONAL BOUNDARY
- RAILWAY LINE
- NATIONAL PARK
- OTHER RESERVES
- SEA OR LAKE

13

Town Plans Town Plans Town Pla

Town Plans Town Plans Town Pla

Durban's high population and clogged roads add to the atmosphere of this hot and steamy seaside city.

Durban Durban Durban Durban

Durban City & Surrounds

Durban is summed-up in one picture ... if you could find it! A Zulu ricksha driver bouncing along the main road, carrying overseas tourists on his vehicle as he passes colonial and Victorian-styled buildings, while in the background colourfully-dressed traditional Indian locals stroll the streets ... while young white boys carry their surfboards to the beach. There's a whole lot of culture and style mixed in together, each rich and authentic, and yet all seemingly at peace with one another.

GOLDEN MILE

Early Portuguese explorers described the coast's sea sand as being 'sands of gold', hence the name the Golden Mile. Populated with towering hotels and skyscrapers, and laced with plenty of eating establishments (from five-star fare down to a quick burger and fries), the Mile is one of Durban's most popular places. Lovers walk hand-in-hand, kids tumble into the beach waves, adults surf or saunter along the beach or the promenade. There's something for everyone, and the warmer water means that you don't need to pluck up any courage to venture into the water. Courage is not a necessary quality on the beachfront, as the shark nets and expert lifesavers on duty make it as safe as possible. From your hotel or any activity spot in town it's a few minutes walk and you're on the beach – end the day with a leisurely paddle in the waves. Aaaah, you might not want to go home again!

SHOP TILL YOU FLOP

Just off Grey Street you'll find a bazaar of colour, tastes, smells and textures in the

Above: *Durban ricksha driver in full dress.*
Below: *An aerial view of the city.*

Originally known as Port Natal, Durban's harbour is the biggest and busiest in Africa, handling 5000 vessels a year and two-thirds of SA's container trade.

Durban

Indian shopping district. Jewellery and trinkets galore will dazzle you as you snake your way through the courtyard bazaars. The Victoria Street Market allows visitors a more typically African shopping experience, with curios and souvenirs (I love Durbs t-shirts and the like) covering a wide range of tastes and budgets, all with the possibility of a negotiated settlement for the bottom line. One thing you won't be able to haggle over, however, is one of Durban's famous bunny chows from one of a string of traditional food-sellers. The popular takeaway treat is made up of half a loaf of bread filled with curry – the insides are pulled out and you use it to soak up the curry sauce.

JUMA MUSJID MOSQUE
Located on Grey Street, the Juma Musjid is the largest mosque in the southern Hemisphere, and its twin minarets dominate Grey Street. Built in 1927, it occupies almost 1000m^2 and can take up to 4500 worshippers at one time. Other mosques worth visiting include the Bayview Muslim Cultural Society Mosque, Overport Mosque, Queens Bridge Mosque, Riverside Soofie Mosque and Mausoleum, Soofie Mosque, Sufi Saheb Badsha Peer Darbar, West Street Mosque and the Zanazibarian Mosque.

BAT CENTRE
An innovative and charitable community arts centre established in 1995, which supports local artists in creating a new and vibrant cultural diversity. The centre's aim is for artists to gain self-respect as well as a valued place in the local community. The public are invited to join in a number of arts-related workshops and activities, as well as enjoying the opportunity to meet the artists in the flesh. There are also many types of classes held here regularly.

FUN IN THE SUN
Minitown is great fun for the kids, but adults will also enjoy being able to walk around like a giant examining the small-scale (1:24) replicas of Durban's famous buildings. Funworld has bumper cars, kiddies rides and some real thrill-rides, like the daunting swing boat.

Above: *Small craft harbour in Durban.*
Below: *Add some flavour to your trip.*

STOP IN FOR A BITE
The Fitzsimons Snake Park (alongside Snake Park Beach!) houses local and exotic species of these scaly creatures. Watch the animals being fed, attend daily demonstrations of venomous snakes, lectures on snakebite management, as well as the chance to 'pet' some non-venomous snakes.

Top Tip
The Natural Science Museum is a must to visit: aside from all its other fascinating displays, the ancient skeleton of a dodo and South Africa's only Egyptian mummy will make the trip worthwhile.

You can stay your own way in Durban, with accommodation on offer that ranges from palatial presidential suites to cosy B&Bs.

Durban Durban Durban Durban

One of Durban's great assets is its accessibility: an hour's flight from Joburg, all the city's attractions are easy to access.

Durban

PLACE OF INTEREST

1. Beachview Mall
2. Automobile Association
3. Whysalls Camera Museum
4. The Wheel (Shopping Mall)
5. Dept of Home Affairs
6. Mauritian Consulate
7. Chinese Consulate
8. Italian Consulate
9. The Playhouse
10. Library
11. Local History Museum
12. Receiver of Revenue
13. Wild Fig Tree (Heritage Site)
14. Tourist Junction
15. City Hall housing: Natural Science Museum, Durban Art Gallery
16. British Consulate
17. Greek Consulate
18. Cambridge College
19. Mozambican Consulate
20. German Consulate
21. American Consulate
22. GA Riches Building
23. St Anthony Catholic Private Aided School

ACCOMMODATION

A. Edward
B. The Balmoral
C. Palm Beach
D. Holiday Inn Garden Court South Beach
E. Lonsdale

19

> Durban's streets are pretty busy and relatively safe during the day ... but wandering around at night will put you at risk of a mugging.

Durban Durban Durban Durban

WALKING THE CITY

It's really easy to take yourself around town (see the recommended tour below), but guided tours are always preferable for the insight provided which you would otherwise miss out on. Durban Africa runs The Oriental Walkabout and the Historical Walkabout. The former is a fascinating stroll past the Juma Musjid Mosque, the historic Grey Street business district, Indian shopping arcades and the Muthi Trade Market, as well as the Emmanuel Cathedral and the market on Victoria Street. The historically inclined route takes in Farewell Square, the Playhouse complex, the statue of Dick King and the Vasco Da Gama clock. Other options are the Victoria Embankment Walking Tour, the Central City Walking Tour and the Golden Mile Tour.

The Esplanade.

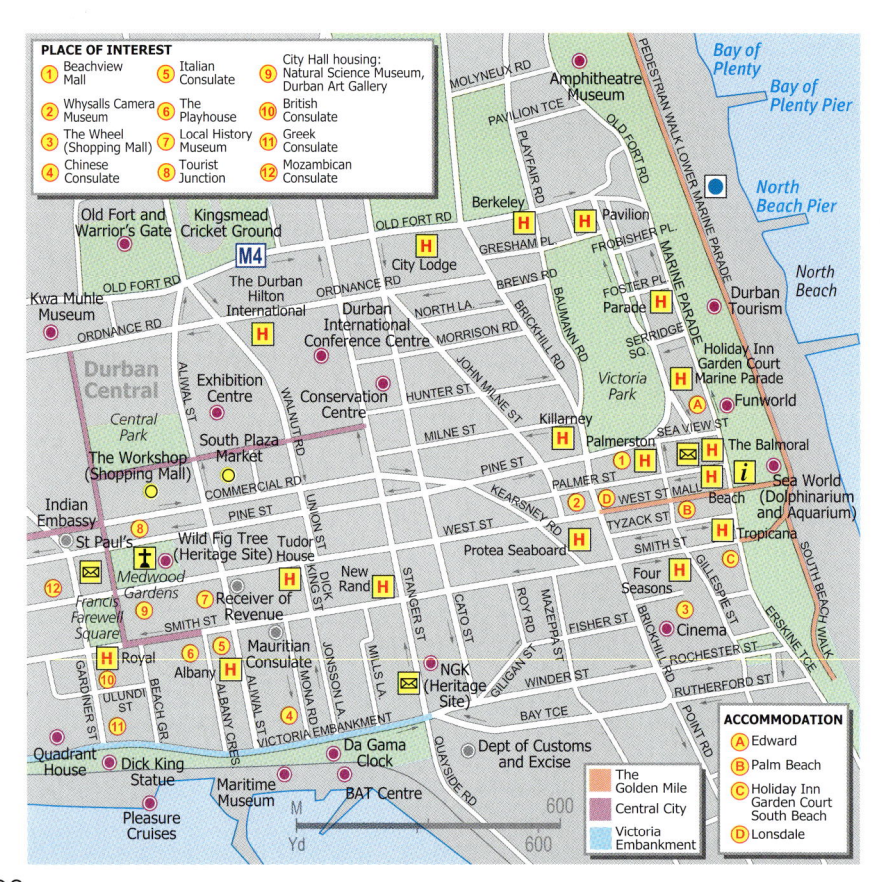

PLACE OF INTEREST

1. Beachview Mall
2. Whysalls Camera Museum
3. The Wheel (Shopping Mall)
4. Chinese Consulate
5. Italian Consulate
6. The Playhouse
7. Local History Museum
8. Tourist Junction
9. City Hall housing: Natural Science Museum, Durban Art Gallery
10. British Consulate
11. Greek Consulate
12. Mozambican Consulate

ACCOMMODATION

A. Edward
B. Palm Beach
C. Holiday Inn Garden Court South Beach
D. Lonsdale

The Golden Mile
Central City
Victoria Embankment

20

Voted the Best Managed City in Africa in 1998, Durban (aka Ethekweni) is the ideal location for a major convention centre.

Durban Durban Durban Durban

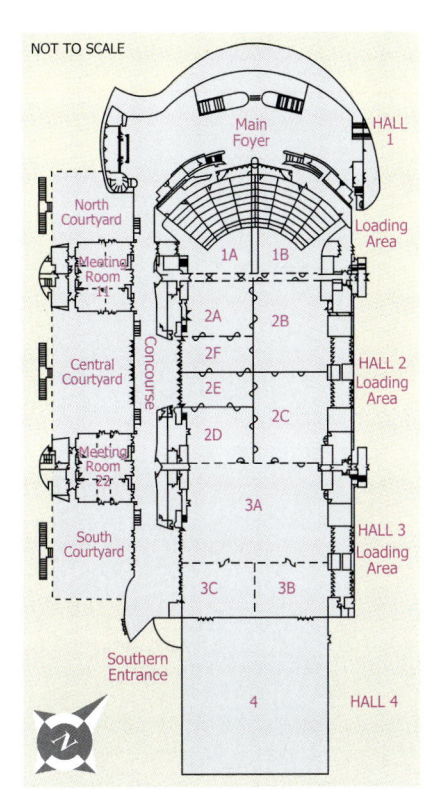

Convention centre at night.

INTERNATIONAL CONVENTION CENTRE

One of the safest spots in South Africa, and superbly run with excellent facilities and hi-tech policing, Durban is proud to proclaim that it is the place where Africa and the world meet ... and there have been numerous major conferences and summits staged here over the last few years. Lying just 20 minutes away from Durban International Airport, the ICC is centrally located along with the beachfront hotels, the CBD and countless local attractions. One of the world's most advanced conference facilities, the ICC is fully air-conditioned and has three main halls that can combine into one massive meeting point to hold 5000 delegates – and if you need 10 000 they'll simply open up the neighbouring Durban Exhibition Centre for you. Hall 1 has seating for 1800 delegates ... and these seats can lift up into the ceiling to create an open floor surface if required.

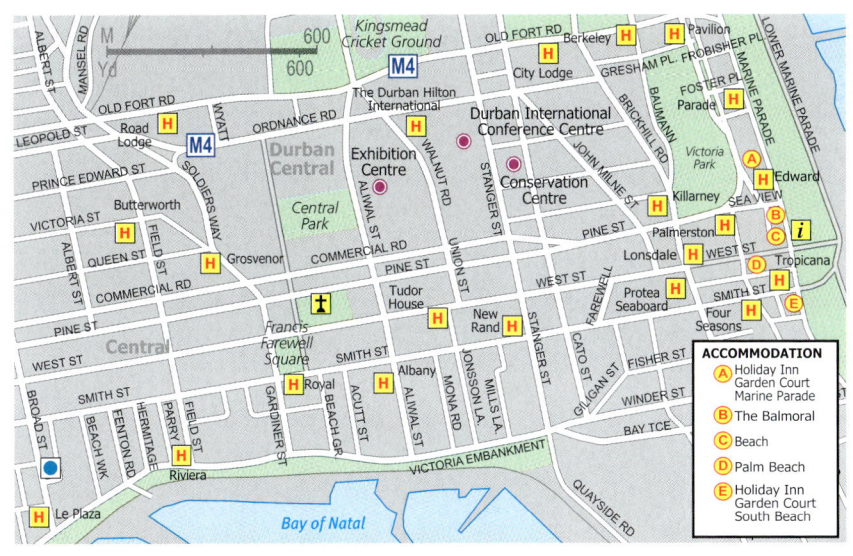

ACCOMMODATION
- A Holiday Inn Garden Court Marine Parade
- B The Balmoral
- C Beach
- D Palm Beach
- E Holiday Inn Garden Court South Beach

Established in 1849, the gardens are Africa's 'longest-blooming' botanical garden ... and possibly the only one to have been visited by lions!

Durban Durban Durban Durban

Frangipani in the botanical gardens.

The Victorian-style visitor's centre harks back to the garden's origins, while the subtropical setting yields stunning arrays of indigenous and exotic fauna. A fragrant garden opens up some of the floral fantasies for blind visitors, while the Nedbank Music at the Lake concerts is another popular drawcard. The tranquil setting of the lake, along with a healthy birdlife, pleasant outside tea garden and stunning orchid house, completes the botanical picture of what has been dubbed 'The City's Brightest Jewel'.

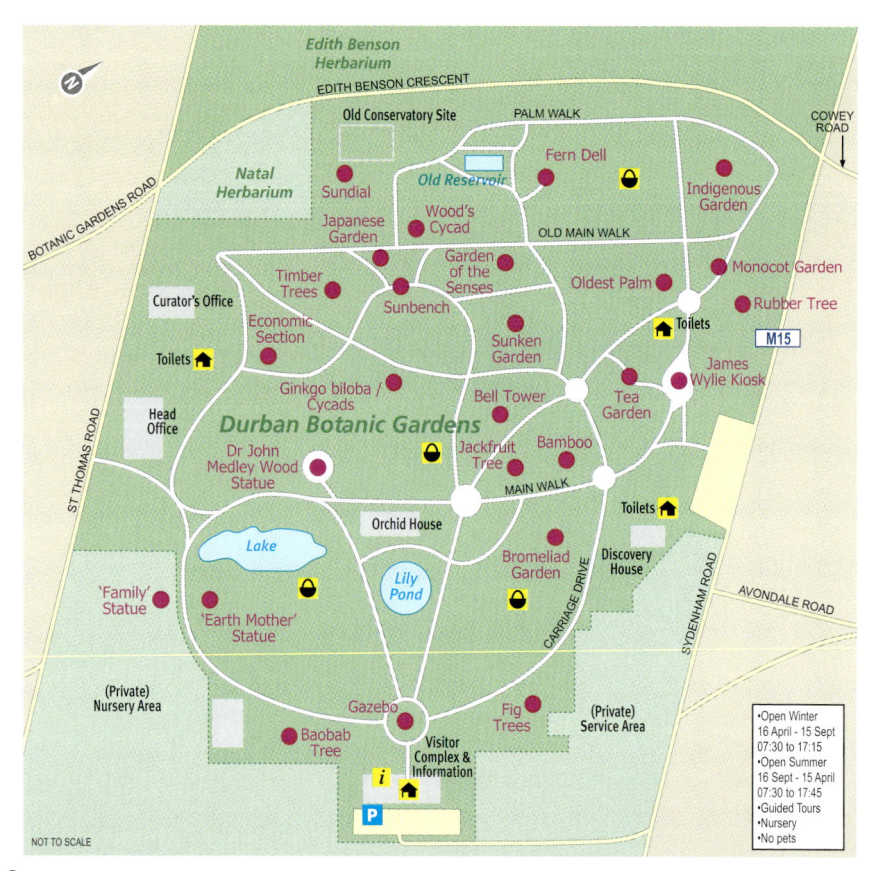

- Open Winter 16 April - 15 Sept 07:30 to 17:15
- Open Summer 16 Sept - 15 April 07:30 to 17:45
- Guided Tours
- Nursery
- No pets

A dolphin show will always turn an unhappy face upside down ... and the seals and penguins will finish it off with a flourish.

Durban Durban Durban Durban

Sure it's going to be Africa's largest marine theme park, as well as amongst the world's Top 10 biggest aquariums (by volume), but what's even more exciting is the lengths the facility goes to educate and rehabilitate. Major education programmes, lectures and tours are offered to inspire future generations towards caring for our marine environment. Sea World's rehabilitation programme cares for injured marine life (of all descriptions) and is Florence Nightingale in its dedication, but the cherry on top is the fact that the water uShaka Marine World pumps into its system from the ocean is actually returned to 'Neptune's Playground' cleaner than when it was first brought in. A drop in the ocean, perhaps, but every bit helps.

uShaka's Marine World theme park is geared towards families in every respect, from the facilities to the design and even the attractions. Set over 16ha, and likely to cost R700-million when completed, the park takes visitors on a half-a-kilometre underwater viewing extravaganza through 7 large aquariums and a separate 25 watery exhibits, proudly showing off its thousands of marine guests who come from well over 200 different families (aka species!). The park also shows off the southern hemisphere's largest shark collection as well as Africa's largest dolphinarium (stocked with the world's biggest aquarium-dwelling dolphins)! A 1200-seater stadium for dolphin watching and a 300-seater for seal enthusiasts offer a real 'wow' and 'ooh' experience. A major drawcard is the snorkel lagoon that gives visitors a chance to 'swim with the fishies' and explore a safe underwater terrain (don't worry – there are no interleading doors to the shark tank). Take a tumble at Wet 'n Wild World – kamikaze-style slides and rides make it impossible to stay dry, while for the more faint of heart there are cozy tube rides and splash pools.

Bottlenose dolphin.

Top Tip

The aquarium holds roughly 17 500 cubic meters of water, making it one of the largest in the world behind Atlantis (28 000), Beijing (20 000), Sea World San Diego and Orlando (both 22 800).

- A USHAKA SEAWORLD
- 1 DOLPHIN STADIUM
- 2 SEAL STADIUM
- 3 SHIPWRECK
- 4 AQUARIUM
- 5 PENGUIN ROOKERY

- B USHAKA WET 'N WILD WORLD
- C TREASURE WORLD
- D SAAMBR & USIM OFFICES

23

Trinkets and curios abound in town ... but if you're planning a trip into the interior then hold off on the shopping spree!

Durban Durban Durban Durban

Variety and spice is what makes shopping in Durban a delight. Major shopping centers filled with exclusive boutiques and the ubiquitous chain store, as well as scores of factory shops ... not to mention the hundreds of small operations that will gladly peddle you anything from fine jewellery, textiles, any number of local arts and crafts, fresh (and deliciously local!) fruit and veg, leatherwork, woodcrafts and even offer repairs to your bicycle! And the prices are generally better than competitive: they're good! It doesn't hurt to indulge in a gentle spot of haggling ... just don't expect sub-continental-like dips in price. Get a bit chipped off the price, smile and pay up. A special treat is a visit to the 11-domed Victoria Street Market, which replaced the old Indian market (fire raised it to the ground in 1973). Found on the corner of Victoria and Russell streets, hundreds of vendors offer up a potpourri of colour and smells, with curries, spices and herbs for sale on the ground floor, while more than 50 stores and a number of restaurants will tempt you on the first floor.

The Gateway Shopping Centre.

Durban doesn't lack when it comes to getting down and boogying, or even just going out on the town for a jolly old meal with friends, family ... or that special someone. The night air is welcoming and the city breathes with a spirit for fun and adventure. There's plenty to choose from and even meagre budgets will find plenty of outlets, but if you have the means then a lavish after-dark feast at one of the must-be-seen-at restaurants will go down like sunflower against a chain-saw. If you have the legs to get down and boogy then a catalogue of vibey and funky night spots will not disappoint.

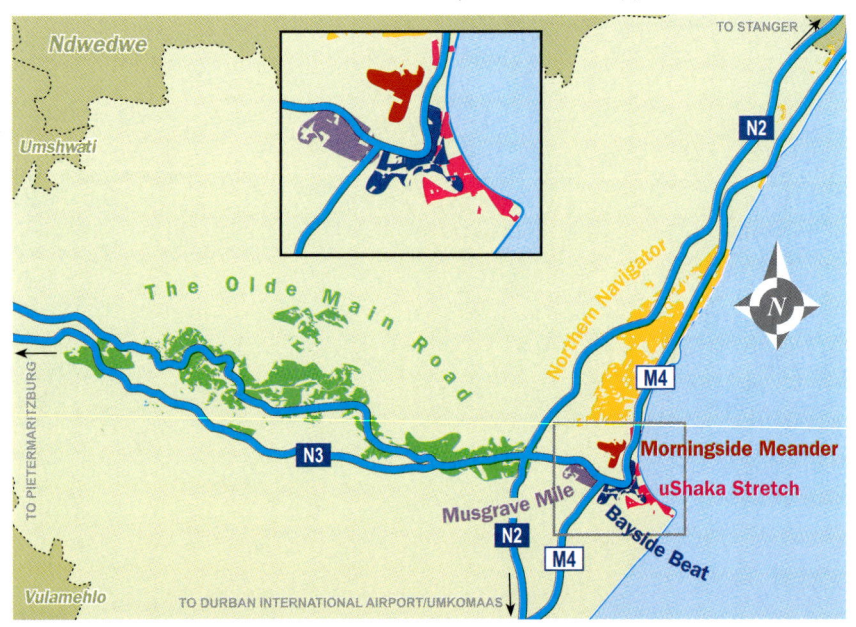

Top Tip
Durban has something of a reputation for the number (not to mention the quality) of its second-hand stores and antique shops: X marks the spot in Durban for antique hunters!

24

Durban's R1,5-billion Suncoast Casino and Entertainment World is a major cog in the city's plans to rejuvenate the city's status as a tourist mecca.

Durban

DURBAN'S HOT SPOTS
Billy the Bum's (trendy restaurant and cocktail bar), BAT Deck in October (live-music bar), Bean Bag Bohemia (live music), Mo Jazz (weekend music), Bar Langoustine by the Sea (popular bar), Butcher Boys (fashionable steakhouse), The Fish Co. Bar (smart bar), The Monkey Bar (Italian cigar and sports bar), Ned Kelly's Irish Bar (a rocking Irish pub), Scallywags (live music bar), Southern Junction (restaurant with bar and music), 'Tall Ships' (upmarket hotel bar), 80s (top-notch nightclub), Blue Bottles Nightclub (waterfront nightclub).

WILSON'S WHARF
Durban's beachfront has been revitalized by the development of the Suncoast Casino and Entertainment World, along with Wilson's Wharf and uShaka Island Marine Theme Park, all of which provide a bright new outlook and opportunities for fun and fancy to locals and tourists alike. Wilson's Wharf offers Durban its first 'dinkum' waterfront complex and boasts a revitalized marina (catering for 75 boats) watched over by thirst-quenching pubs, as well as restaurants, speciality shops and a craft market, all woven together with characteristic boardwalks.

Wilson's Wharf Waterfront at night.

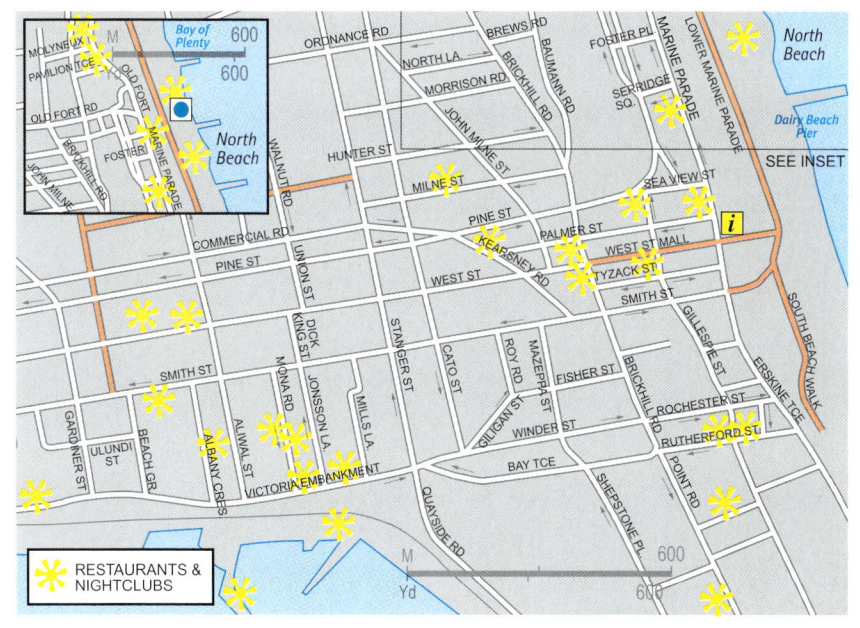

25

Aside from the beauty of seeing these magnificent creatures 'in the feather', the sight of them in their natural habitats will give you goose-flesh.

Durban Durban Durban Durban Du

UMGENI RIVER BIRD PARK
Acknowledged as one of the world's top three bird parks, Umgeni boasts more than 3000 species of bird, with indigenous and exotic varieties in abundance. Visitors walk through massive aviaries boasting waterfalls and a wide range of vegetation to make the birds feel right at home. The highlight of your visit will be the twice-daily free flight show in which the birds float around you in their own sweet way, encouraging you to consider the value of conservation.

BEACHWOOD MANGROVE SWAMP
Lying at the mouth of the Mgeni River, this natural national monument is a rare mangrove swamp, forest and estuary, creating a remarkable habitat for birds ... but fortunately not being home to insects that like to bite humans, making for a more enjoyable visit to this habitat with its bird hide, picnic spots and activity centre.

A parrot at the Umgeni River Bird Park.

Inanda, a peaceful rural area near Durban, was the closest area to the city where non-whites could buy land, thus Zulus and Indians became neighbours.

Durban Durban Durban Durban

Gandhi statue.

INANDA HERITAGE ROUTE
The much-vaunted Inanda Heritage Route kicks off at the Ohlange Institute, the place where President Nelson Mandela historically cast his first-ever vote (in the 1994 elections). A school stands there to this day, as well as the grave of ANC hero John Dube.

Next stop is Phoenix, the settlement where Mahatma Gandhi found the inspiration to develop his ground-breaking strategy of resistance to oppression, the philosophy of passive resistance. This policy was to have a major effect on the world's socio-political relations. Gandhi (the suburb's most famous former resident) spent 21 years working in South Africa – he came here after learning of the legal hassles experienced by Indian immigrants. Gandhi's restored home has been rededicated as a monument to the socially sacred concepts of peace and justice. One of Africa's oldest girls-only private schools, the Inanda Seminary was started back in 1869 by Mary Edwards, a missionary, and it went on to guide and teach many of South Africa's greatest black women leaders in politics and business.

Ebuhleni gives visitors a chance to dip into the Shembe Church and its religious past and present, which began in 1913 when Isiah Shembe was guided by a voice from the Heavens, instructing him on the laws of the Shembe Church and on plans to build the order's holy church.

Top Tip
In 1904, Gandhi bought a small farm called Phoenix, where he set up a community which operated on the principles of co-operation and sharing.

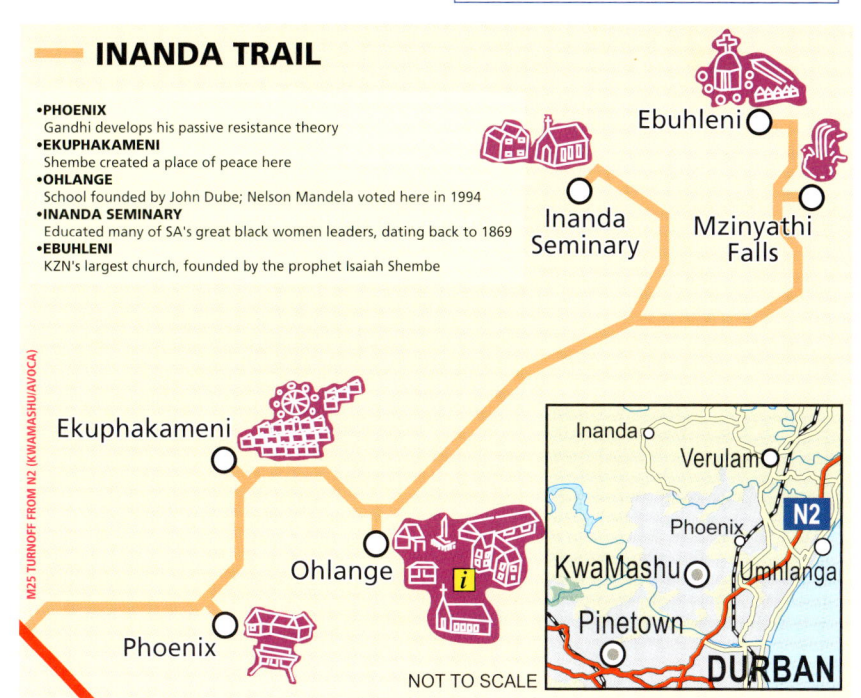

INANDA TRAIL
- **PHOENIX**
  Gandhi develops his passive resistance theory
- **EKUPHAKAMENI**
  Shembe created a place of peace here
- **OHLANGE**
  School founded by John Dube; Nelson Mandela voted here in 1994
- **INANDA SEMINARY**
  Educated many of SA's great black women leaders, dating back to 1869
- **EBUHLENI**
  KZN's largest church, founded by the prophet Isaiah Shembe

NOT TO SCALE

27

Durban's 3-million population makes up 35% of KZN's population ... all living on just 1.5% of the province's land.

Durban Durban Durban Durban Du

Brilliantly decorated meditation room.

THE TEMPLE OF UNDERSTANDING
Located on Florence Nightingale Drive in the Indian suburb of Chatsworth (opposite the Chatsworth Centre), the Temple of Understanding is the spiritual home of Indians as well as members of the Hare Krishna faith (it's the largest Hare Krishna temple in the Southern Hemisphere). Built as recently as 1985, the temple is an architectural marvel with gold-tipped steeples and an ornate marble temple room, an inner sanctuary, all of which will be revealed to you on the guided tour around this breathtaking temple with its surrounding moat and gardens. Leave enough time in your trip to indulge in a delicious veggie meal (which won't break the bank) in the temple's canteen. There are plenty of Hindu temples to visit driving along the Umgeni Road, but the Shree Ambalavaanar Alayam Hindu Temple (890 Bellair Road, Cato Manor) is reached by a more enjoyable drive through an area with a sad history of forced removals. Brightly painted images of Ganesha, Shiva and Vishnu decorate the walls of this national monument that harks back to 1875! The annual Hindu firewalking festival is held here every March ... so start practising!

Top Tip
Durban's many green lungs include Pigeon Valley (a Natural Heritage Park loved by birders and hikers) and the 220ha Silverglen, which has within it Africa's first medical plants nursery.

28

To cope with the huge urban population, more than 30 nature reserves have been established within a 10-mile radius of the city centre.

Durban

Durban's building boom of the 1980s saw the demolition of countless historic buildings, but local conservationists (MOSS) preserved vital 'green lungs'.

Durban Durban Durban Durban Du

KENNETH STAINBANK NR
A 253ha reserve plonked down amidst the city of Durban's suburbs. A birdwatcher's paradise and a great place to learn about the effect man has had on the nature around which he has built his cities, the reserve offers 13km of walks, even catering for the physically challenged. Night drives bring nocturnal mammals and birds into view, while day delights include bushbuck, duiker and the majestic impala and zebra.

KRANTZKLOOF NATURE RESERVE
Located in the suburb of Kloof (under 30km outside of Durban, between Pinetown and Hillcrest), Krantzkloof is found in the thick forests of the gorge cut by the Emolweni River and is a great example of grasslands and coastal forests. This relatively large reserve contains many trails that take visitors into the gorge (kloof) with its three waterfalls (the biggest of which thunders down from a height of 90m).

BLUFF NATURE RESERVE
Proclaimed in October 1974 in the suburb of Bluff, BNR spreads over just 45ha and is made up of a large pan, with a forest alongside it. The pan is home sweet home for countless waterbirds and waders, with two bird hides allowing visitors great close-ups of anything from spoonbills to cormorants. A self-guided trail drifts around the edge of the pan, showcasing the diverse birdlife that enjoys the reserve, while a number of mammal species have also been spotted, among them monkeys, genets, mongoose, shrews, moles and rats.

Rock & Water Monitors, common in the nature reserves around Durban.

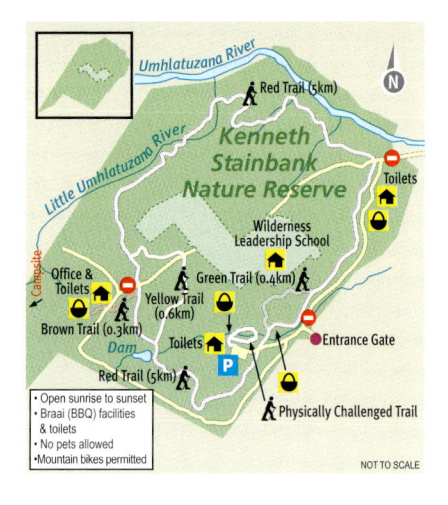

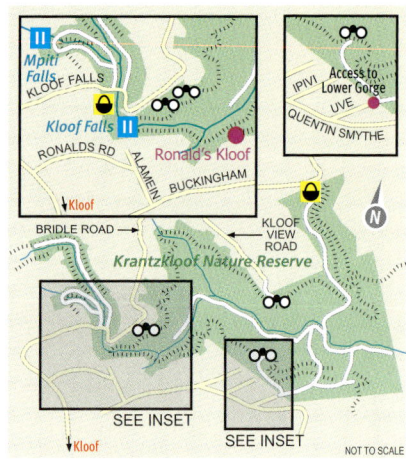

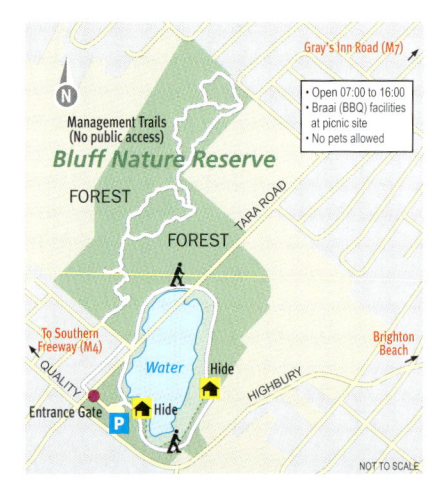

30

MOSS protects wilderness areas within Durban's suburbs, with more than 20 reserves within easy reach of the city centre.

Durban

OTHER RESERVES

Morningside's Burman Bush Nature Reserve (50ha) is a pristine patch of coastal bushland that has grown its own way since the mid 1800s. Alive with vervet monkeys and coursed by three trails (all conveniently colour co-ordinated!), Silverglen Nature Reserve is the biggest area of public land in the city limits. Made up of open coastal grasslands as well as dense bush, Silverglen was a formerly popular reserve laced with hiking trails ... but regrettably its current status seems unsafe. The Shongweni Resources Reserve is the biggest of the local nature reserves, and what it lacks in mammal species it makes up for in its birdlife. Visitors can enjoy more than 15km of hiking trails, which offer up amazing views of interesting rocks carved over the centuries by the elements.

The resident Black Sparrowhawk of Pigeon Valley.

31

Lying on the N3 heading towards Pietermaritzburg, Pinetown spreads over part of the famous Comrades Marathon route.

Durban

PINETOWN

The Pinetown Museum displays with pride representations of Pinetown's earliest settlers, from stone-age man through to the settlers who started cultivating the land and erecting dwellings, as well as modern man in all his and her glory. The museum has a wide range of cultural artifacts and a big collection of historical photographs for visitors to sneak a peak at, as well as a model of a Zulu warrior. OK, so it's not Madame Tussauds ... but get your pic taken next to him anyway! Pinetown's Japanese Garden is a 4.5ha park of rolling lawns and indigenous plants and is a very popular family venue: the children's playground and park is overlooked by the delicious tea garden.

Top Tip
The gorgeous scenery around Fields Hill belies the toil Comrades' runners endure to reach it. Take the car if you prefer ...

THE MARIANNHILL MONASTERY

The Mariannhill Monastery was established in 1882 by East European Trappist monks and remains a working monastery to this day, employed in the skills of embroidery, carpentry and with a shop open to the public. There is also a fantastic book printer and binder (bring your old family bibles here for repair). The lovely tea garden also offers hikes catering for between 70 to 140 people ... with lunch or supper thrown in. Hikes go down into a nearby farm and into the valley. Fascinating tours through the huge repository are also run regularly. The brothers who work at the monastery are normal human beings who roll up their sleeves and help out wherever they're needed, washing dishes or doing whatever is required; they don't walk around in brown cloths with their hands clasped ... but they do operate on Monastery time! The Monastery's Sunday morning services are open to the public.

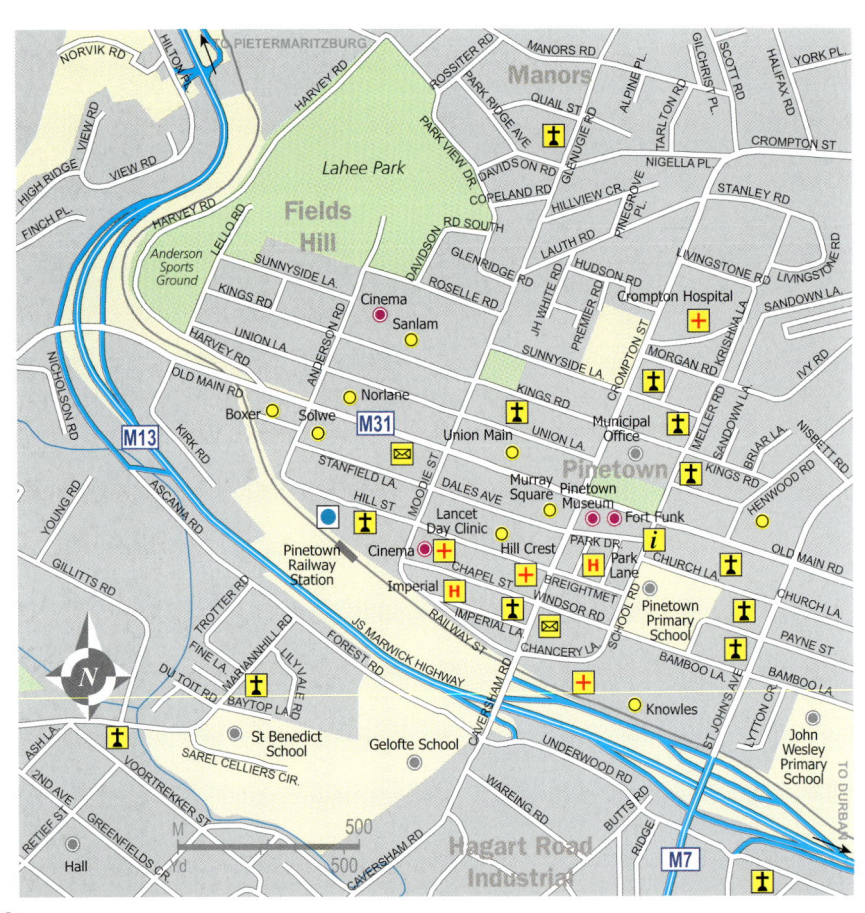

32

Two kilometres south of Pinetown is the beautiful Mariannhill Monastery set under giant umkhulu trees in the 'valley of the monks'.

Durban

GENERAL
South Africa Tourism 011 778 8000
South Africa online www.southafrica.net

KwaZulu-Natal Tourism Authority
031 366 7500, tkzn@iafrica.com,
www.zulu.org.za
031 304 7144, www.tourism-kzn.org
Durban Airport Office 031 408 1000
Cape Town V&A Waterfront 021 405 4540
Customer careline 086 010 1099

Durban Africa (tourism information)
031 304 4934, funinsun@iafrica.com,
www.durbanexperience.co.za,
www.durban.kzn.org.za
www.bookabedahead.co.za

Natal Sharks Board 031 566 0400

Weather Bureau 082 231 1603
Durban International Airport Flight Information
031 451 6669 / 6
Airports Company of SA Management
031 451 6666
Airport Shuttle Bus 031 465 1606 / 1600
Virginia Airport Durban 031 563 7101 / 4
Oribi Airport, Pietermaritzburg Flight
Information 033 386 9286 / 9287
Richards Bay Airport, Zululand Flight
Information SA Express 035 786 0301 / 2
Margate Airport, South Coast Flight
Information SA Airlink 039 317 3267
Ulundi Airport Flight Information SA Link
035 870 1030
Joburg International Airport 011 921 6262

TRANSPORT
Automobile Association (AA) 031 265 0437
Provincial Help Centre 0800 339 911
National Roads 033 392 8100

PUBLIC BUS TRANSPORT
Durban Transport 031 309 5942 / 3 / 4126
Baz Bus 031 304 9099
Cheetah Coaches 033 342 0266
Margate Mini Coaches 039 312 1406
Sani Pass Carriers, Pietermaritzburg
033 701 1017
Umhlanga Express Mini Bus Services
082 268 0651 / 083 440 8650

RAIL INFORMATION
Shosholoza Long Distance Travel
0860 008 888
Spoornet General Enquiries 031 361 3388
Metrorail 031 361 7609

ACCOMMODATION
City Lodge 0800 11 37 90
Holiday Inn 0800 11 77 11
Protea Hotels 0861 11 90 00
Southern Sun 0800 11 77 11

HOTELS IN DURBAN
Albany Hotel 031 304 4381
albany@iafrica.com, www.albanyhotel.co.za
Balmoral Hotel 031 368 5940
balmore@icon.co.za, www.raya-hotels.com
Beach Hotel 031 337 5511
www.goodersonleisure.com
Bellair Hotel 031 465 6865
bellairhotel@worldonline.co.za
Blue Waters Hotel 031 332 4272
www.bluewatershotel.co.za
Britannia Hotel 031 303 2266
britannia@eastcoast.co.za
City Lodge Durban 031 332 1447
cidurb.res@citylodge.co.za
Comfort Lodge 031 368 4611
Fernleigh Gardens Residential Hotel
031 313 4500, fernleigh@telkomsa.net
Holiday Inn Durban Elangeni 031 362 1300
holidayinndurban@southernsun.com
Holiday Inn Garden Court Marine Parade
031 337 3341
higcdbnmarineparade@southernsun.com
Holiday Inn Garden Court North Beach
031 332 7361
higcdbnnorthbeach@southernsun.com
Hotel California 031 303 1146
Hotel Formule 1 031 301 1551
www.hotelformule1.co.za
Killarney Hotel 031 337 4285
Parade Hotel 031 337 4565
res@paradehotel.co.za
www.paradehotel.co.za
Pavilion Hotel 031 337 7366
Protea Hotel Edward 031 337 3681
reservations@proteaedward.co.za
Protea Hotel Landmark Lodge Durban
031 337 3601 www.proteahotels.com
Quarters Hotel 031 303 5246
quarters@icon.co.za, www.quarters.co.za
Riviera Hotel 031 301 3681
funhot@mweb.co.za
Road Lodge Durban 031 304 8202
www.citylodge.co.za
The Hilton Durban 031 336 8100
dbnhilton@icon.co.za, www.hilton.com
The Palace Hotel 031 332 8351
The Royal Hotel 031 333 6000
hotel@theroyal.co.za, www.theroyal.co.za
Travellers Lodge 031 467 3839
Tropicana Hotel 031 368 1511
tropican@iafrica.com
Tudor House Hotel 031 337 7328

EMERGENCY SERVICES
Police 10111
Ambulance 10177
Fire Department 031 361 0000
Emergency Chemist 031 209 3456
Tourist Protection Unit 031 368 4453
Mountain Rescue Services 031 307 7744
Sea Rescue Services 031 332 9772
Breakdowns (AA) 0800 010 101

The Dolphin Coast is named for the proliferation of bottle-nosed dolphins that scout along this stretch of coastline.

North Coast

The Dolphin Coast Region

Sugarcane fields.

The North Coast is like a holidaymaker's goldmine: spectacular watersport-friendly beaches, fringed by indigenous dunes and forests, while inland are found rolling sugar-cane plantations, the white gold of KwaZulu-Natal. Blythedale and Zinkwazi beaches are popular watersport and bird-watching spots. Nearby Stanger (an economic hotspot, known for its lush hillside and resultant early morning blanket of mist) is the final resting-place of the great Zulu chief, Shaka, with kraals, a monument and a memorial garden honouring his life. The Tugela River is watched over by a number of forts and war graves dating back to the 1879 Anglo-Zulu War.

VERULAM AND TONGAAT
Over 150-years old, the town of Verulam (the province's third oldest) is spread across hilly terrain above the Umdloti River.
La Mercy Beach is pretty, safe and within sight of the wave-riding dolphins. The spirit of the east is big in town: Verulam Market offers a gastronomic experience, while many Hindu temples in town provide an historic feel. The Hazelmere Resource Reserve is a fabulous picnic and watersport venue in the countryside offering good facilities.
With its rich sugar harvesting tradition, Tongaat lies on the Sugar Coast, one of the sweetest districts in the world! The town was named after the Tongati River (meaning snuff box tree river), and its birth was a result of the need to house the sugar 'pickers'. A couple of awesome Indian temples, scenic drives, the Maidstone Mill and the Maidstone Country Club, and the Dudley Pringle Dam should sort out most visitors' needs. If crocs are more your thing, then slink into Crocodile Creek, home to thousands of Nile crocs and similar slithering creatures (leave the Speedo at home for this visit).

Top Tip
The remains of a stone age sea shell at the lagoon mouth will delight the unsuspecting stroller along the Umhlanga Lagoon Nature Reserve.

The Sugar Coast is known as The Gateway to Paradise, and Umhlanga occupies top billing on this magnificent coastline.

Umhlanga

A top-class resort town, the Umhlanga ('place of reeds') offers a great beach with a 2,7km promenade for joggers and walkers, the historic 21m-tall landmark lighthouse, Granny's Pool and a natural shelter popular with fishermen and launchers of ski boats. The town is an arts and crafts haven and also offers all the best holiday fun: ten-pin bowling, water-sports, golf, bowls, fishing, diving and even pony and horse riding, while the Gateway shopping centre is one of the biggest in the southern Hemisphere. Hawaan Nature Reserve (4km outside of Umhlanga Rocks) offers guided walks in a well-established coastal forest with rare trees and birdlife, and the Umhlanga Lagoon Nature Reserve has a well-trodden lagoon and dune trails through coastal forest teeming with birds and small mammals.

The lighthouse on Umhlanga Beach.

1. Umhlanga Plaza
2. Riley Centre
3. Hillcon Centre
4. Granada Centre
5. Chartwell Centre
6. Municipal Office
7. Municipal Clinic
8. Post Office

35

Ballito lures fishermen like sharks to an extra-raw steak, while divers and spearfishermen can enjoy a magnificent reef setting.

Ballito Ballito Ballito Ballito Ballito B

Formerly a gentle little resort town, Ballito (along with Salt Rock and Shaka's Rock) is undergoing tourist and development explosions. Willard Beach is one of Ballito's top attractions for sun-worshippers, although other popular sandy spots include Clarke Bay, the Ballito tidal pool and Salmon Bay (thumbs up from the surfers). Two excellent golf courses will keep the long-stick brigade happy: the Umhlali Country Club is located in exquisite settings and features a resident zebra, while Zimbali combines beauty with a tough challenge on this Tom Weiskopf-designed course overlooking the coastline. If you've got the stomach for heights, why not brave the skies and microlight along the Dolphin Coast. You're guaranteed of uninterrupted views, and the old excuse of not knowing how doesn't cut the mustard here: the Dolphin Coast Microlight School will give you the low-downs on how to fly-high.

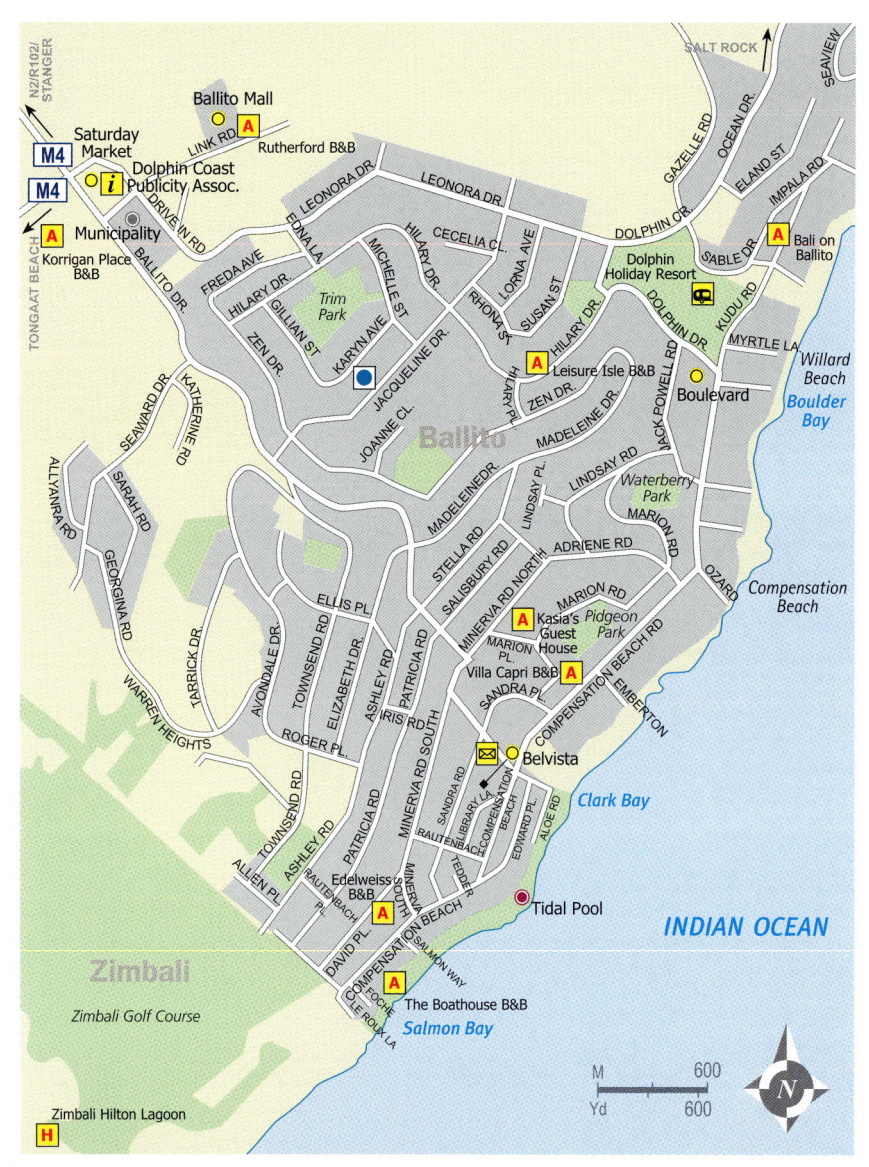

36

Shaka's Rock is an excellent location for fishing as well as snorkelling, notably at Tiffany's Reef and Sheffield Reef.

Shaka's Rock Shaka's Rock Shaka'

Shaka's Rock, today a popular holiday spot.

Shaka's Rock is reputed to be the spot where Shaka had his enemies hurled off the cliff and into the sea ... as well as being his favourite spot to 'be beside the seaside'. Thompson Bay has a hollowed out rock that was believed to have been the king's permanent 'deck chair'. Serviced by a popular tidal pool – and with great viewpoints at Shaka's and Black rocks – Shaka's Rock is a popular seaside resort with plenty of modern timeshare apartments, holiday homes and general accommodation. A great, long stretch of sandy beach offers excellent and safe bathing, surfing, angling ... as well as allowing you to simply bask in the bright, warm glory of the Dolphin Coast.

The nearby Shaka's Kraal is a delightful and authentic village bedecked with Muslim and Hindu architecture. This town with one street occupies the land that formed part of KwaHlomendlini, which was Shaka's royal military homestead.

Top Trip

Just outside Salt Rock lies the town of Umhlali with its Flag Farm animal farm, offering kids and adults a morning of farmyard fun. Feed the animals, get fresh milk from a cow, and enjoy close-up experiences with Fresian workhorses and Welsh ponies, as well as a range of exotic birds and usual furry farm fellows.

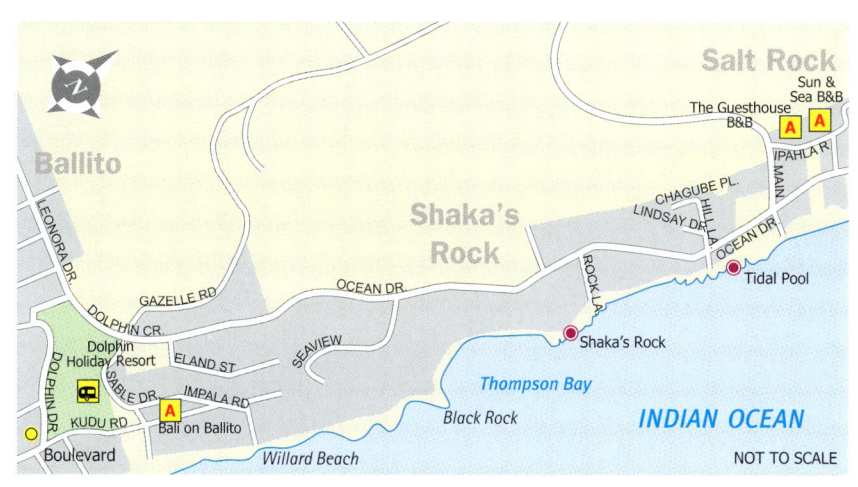

37

One of the oldest clubs in the country, Salt Rock Country Club welcomes visitors keen on a spot of bowls, tennis, squash or swimming.

Salt Rock Salt Rock Salt Rock Salt

Salt Rock earned its name in Shaka's day – his lovely handmaidens would languidly stroll onto the rocks at low tide and harvest all the sea salt left over from the tide. This salt would then be used to barter for much-needed goods from the Colonial settlers as well as traders passing through the area. Salt Rock also has its own popular tidal pool, and lifeguards scour the beach all week with their mission to ensure safe swimming and fun in the sun. The beach has great fishing spots and a selection of great offshore reefs to keep divers' heads down. If you're keen to rough it, the caravan park is little more than a five-iron away from the beach. Oh, for that morning stretch and deep breath of sea air without breaking the bank for the privilege!

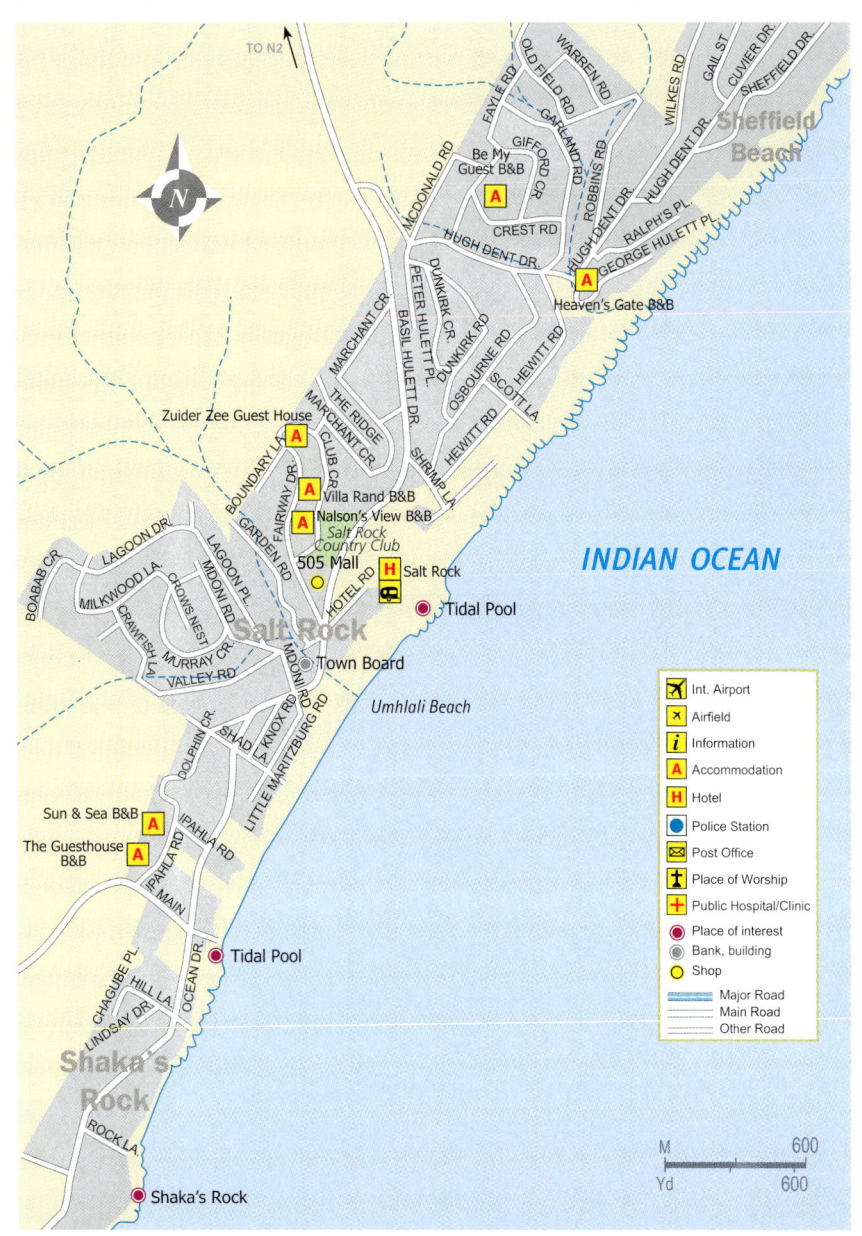

The cemetery found at the Gingindlovu battle site pays homage to the soldiers who lost their lives in the hostilities.

Gingindlovu Gingindlovu Gingindlovu

A small little village encircled by vast fields of sugarcane, Gingindlovu means "swallower of the elephant" in the Zulu tongue, but for the colonial settlers it was more like "swallower of the foreign tongue". Most of the colonial 'visitors' struggled to make a reasonable sound out of pronouncing the name, often light-heartedly referring to it as "Gin-Gin I Love You". Gingindlovu was the site of a military kraal run by Cetshwayo … the same man who won a famous battle against his halfbrother Mbulazi and his warriors at Ndondakusuka. That victory allowed him to claim control of the Zulu Kingdom. The famous Battle of Gingindlovu (2 April, 1879) was the result of one of Cetshwayo's regiments of 11,000 impis attacking 6000 British forces who were approaching Eshowe (the town was then under siege from Zulu warriors). The British drove the Zulus away and brought to an end two months of attrition and isolation.

Monument to the famous Battle of Gingindlovu.

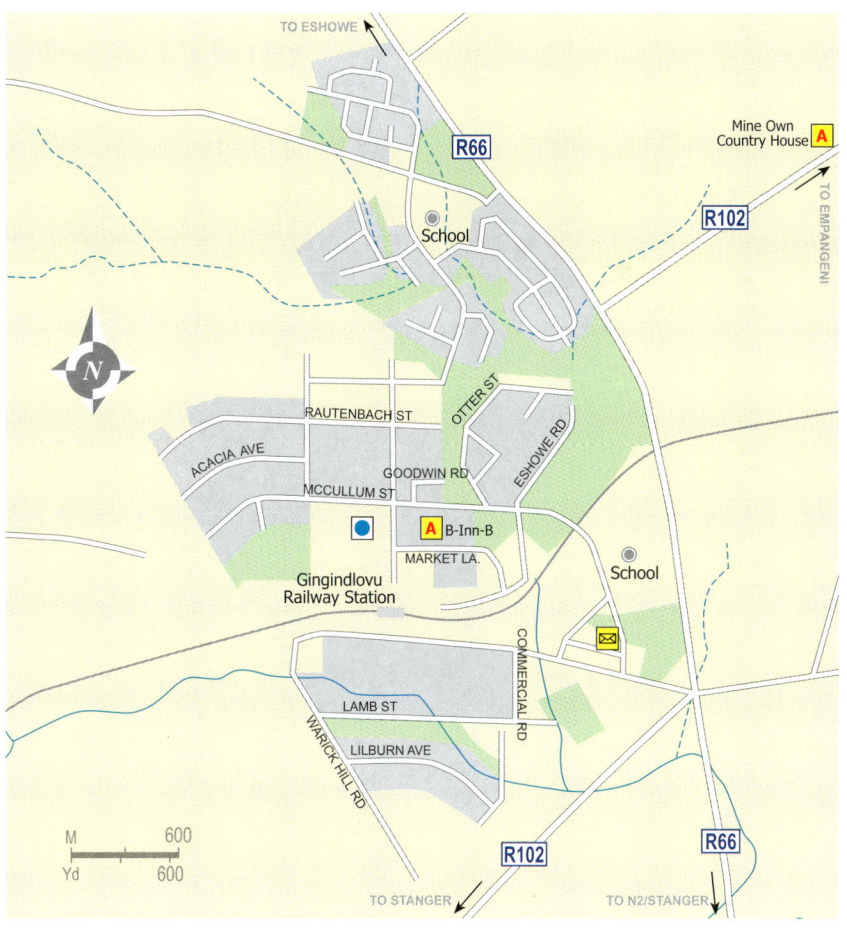

39

Mtunzini means "the shady place", which aptly describes this gorgeous resort town lying at the mouth of the Umlalazi River.

Mtunzini Mtunzini Mtunzini Mtunzi

MTUNZINI
Mtunzini is set in a wild region of coastal forest and mangrove swamps, but the country club offers tennis, squash and a 9-hole golf course. John Dunn, the former adviser to Zulu chief Cetshwayo, lived here with his army of wives: almost 50 in total, grossing a total of 117 children – so there's definitely something to be said for the sea breeze and the ocean views!

UMLALAZI NATURE RESERVE
Lying at the northern point of the Amatikulu Nature Reserve (big game and forested dunes), Umlalazi is big enough to host a few hundred people. The fishing is great, and watersports enthusiasts can really let their hair down, even though the beach isn't 'protected' by shark nets. Long, tropical beaches, lagoon and mangrove swamps are all great 'out of season', while twitchers needing to still tick off the wooly-necked stork or palmnut vulture will be busy!

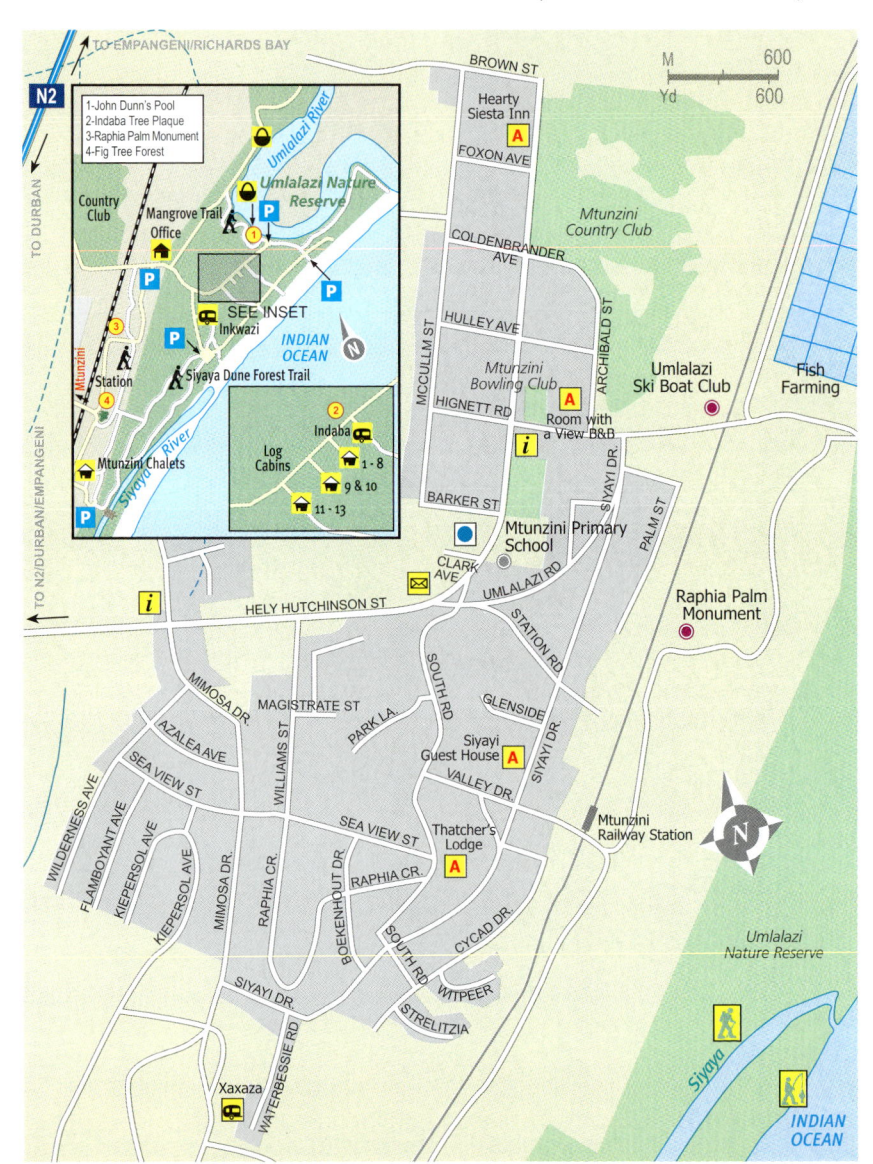

On a plateau protected from the sub-tropical humidity, Eshowe was a popular 'holiday destination' for centuries of successive Zulu kings.

and inland to.. Eshowe Eshowe Eshowe

Eshowe has an interesting history dating from 1860 when missionary settlers from Norway established the KwaMondi Mission. Later Fort Eshowe was built around the mission and was the scene, during the Anglo-Zulu War, of forces under Colonel Pearston being besieged for 10 weeks in 1879. The name KwaMondi was derived from the Zulu name given to Ommund C Oftebro, the first pastor of the Norwegian Mission.

During King Shaka's rule Coward's Bush was the spot where suspected cowards had their courage and resolve tested ... while defeated soldiers were executed at this same place. The spot is now flagged for visitors by the presence of a National Monument Council plaque at an old Kei apple tree.

A fine collection of Zulu arts and crafts is housed at Vukani Museum and Fort Nonqai is now an excellent museum housing a great number of Zulu cultural items, one of which is a replica of the beer mug Queen Victoria gave to King Cetsh.

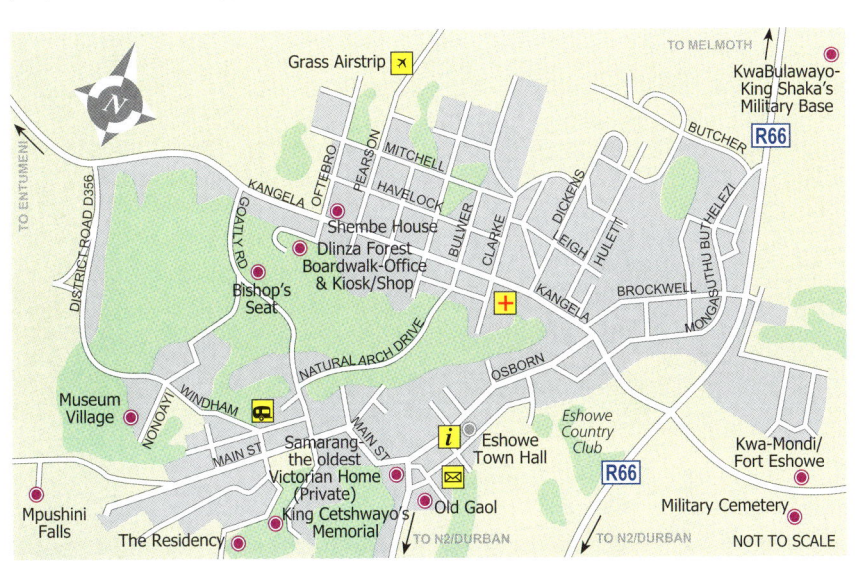

Eshowe Zulu settlement.

Zululand occupies a wildly diverse terrain and offers a wide variety of excellent game and nature reserves.

Zululand & Surrounds

North Coast Region & Maputaland

Spreading from the Tugela River up north to the border of Mozambique, Zululand was formerly ruled by the great Zulu warrior king, Shaka. Great wars and battles were fought in the 19th century between the Zulus and the British, and the Voortrekkers also got involved in hostilities against both sides. The wonderful culture of the Zulu nation is on show at museums such as uMgundgundlovu (Dingane's capital) and Ondini Museum situated at Ulundi, as well as Eshowe's Fort Nonqai. The Greater St Lucia Wetland Park and the Maputaland Marine Reserve are interesting conservation areas, and along the coast there are beautiful beaches, with Lake Sibaya, Kosi Bay and Sodwana Bay all well worth a visit. For tourists there is the pleasure of swimming, scuba diving, surfing and snorkelling in the warm Indian Ocean waters, with deep-sea game fishing for anglers. Game parks in this region are renowned, numbered amongst them the famous Hluhluwe-Umfolozi, whose incredible effort in saving the white rhino has been a major feather in their conservation cap. For keen game watchers a visit to other reserves such as Mkuzi, Ithala and Ndumo is recommended. Tourists can also elect to visit the more exclusive private game reserves - there is plenty of accommodation to please all sorts of personal requirements and individual budgets (ranging from the bold to the pitiful!).

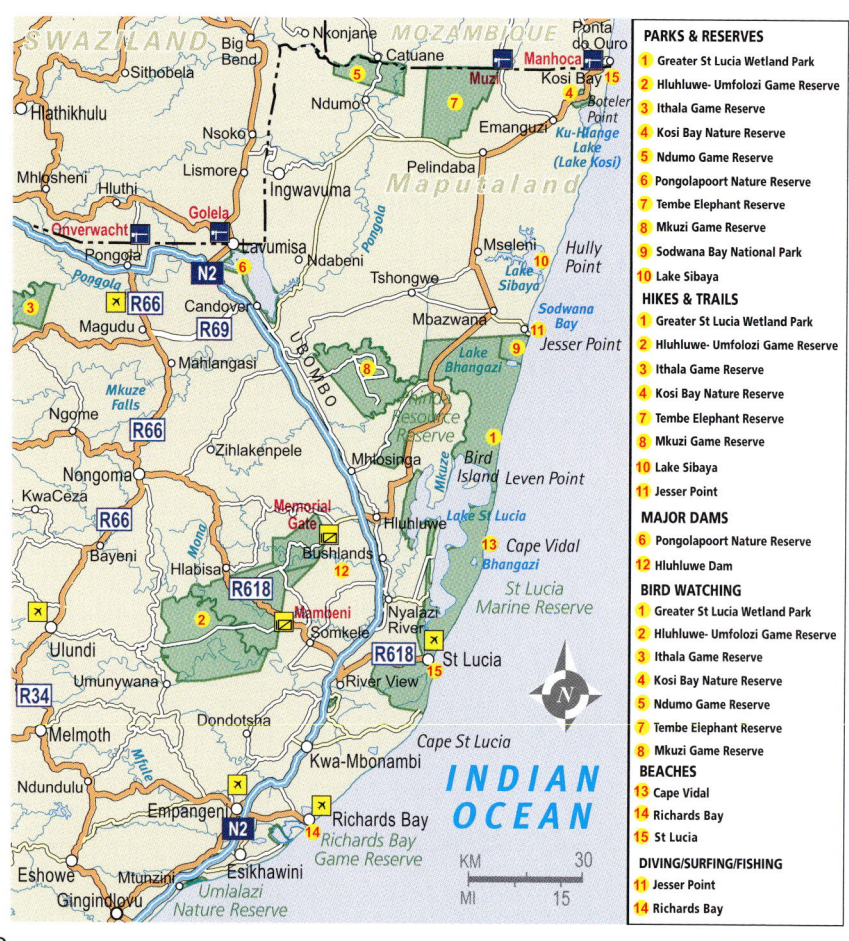

PARKS & RESERVES
1. Greater St Lucia Wetland Park
2. Hluhluwe- Umfolozi Game Reserve
3. Ithala Game Reserve
4. Kosi Bay Nature Reserve
5. Ndumo Game Reserve
6. Pongolapoort Nature Reserve
7. Tembe Elephant Reserve
8. Mkuzi Game Reserve
9. Sodwana Bay National Park
10. Lake Sibaya

HIKES & TRAILS
1. Greater St Lucia Wetland Park
2. Hluhluwe- Umfolozi Game Reserve
3. Ithala Game Reserve
4. Kosi Bay Nature Reserve
7. Tembe Elephant Reserve
8. Mkuzi Game Reserve
10. Lake Sibaya
11. Jesser Point

MAJOR DAMS
6. Pongolapoort Nature Reserve
12. Hluhluwe Dam

BIRD WATCHING
1. Greater St Lucia Wetland Park
2. Hluhluwe- Umfolozi Game Reserve
3. Ithala Game Reserve
4. Kosi Bay Nature Reserve
5. Ndumo Game Reserve
7. Tembe Elephant Reserve
8. Mkuzi Game Reserve

BEACHES
13. Cape Vidal
14. Richards Bay
15. St Lucia

DIVING/SURFING/FISHING
11. Jesser Point
14. Richards Bay

42

Empangeni is named after the mpange tree that grows so prolifically alongside the Mpangeni River that curls through town.

Empangeni

Empangeni, situated in the very beautiful Mpangeni Valley, is an important town for the sugarcane plantations and timber growing industry in the area. It is also a treasure trove for visitors keen to shop for the beautiful crafted work produced by the talented local craftsmen and women. Specially recommended are the Empangeni Arts & Crafts Centre and Jabulani Crafts, the latter created by a local group of handicapped people. For a cultural journey visit the Empangeni Art & Cultural Museum, which has fascinating displays, mainly depicting Zulu culture and history. One of South Africa's largest sugar mills also worth visiting when passing through this area – the Felixton Mill is located only a short way from Empangeni.

Trade store in Empangeni.

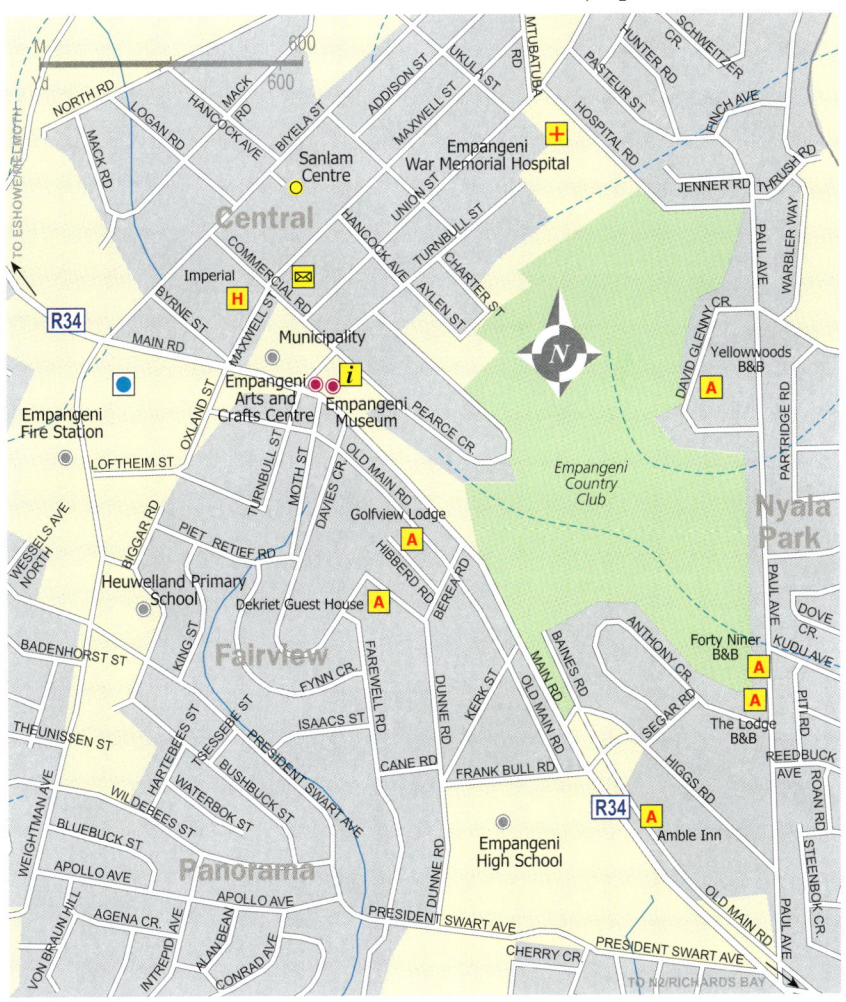

43

Not the winner of the Most Beautiful or Most Charming town award, Richards Bay is instead a perfect base for visiting KZN's top nature reserves.

Richards Bay

A major port serving a large industrial area, Richards Bay offers mining and industrial tours – play to your strengths, they always say. The Richards Bay Game Reserve (under 300ha) on the Mhlatuzi Lagoon looks after the burgeoning birdlife population that draws twitchers from far and wide. The lagoon is famous as the spot where the largest croc in SA history was shot (by John Dunne, 1891), as well as being the kick-off spot for Huberta the hippo's famous east coast trek. The Enseleni Nature Reserve has two trails, the Inkonkoni (7km, over a raised platform walkway across swamp, game and grassland) and the Mvuba (4km), both of which flirt with the Enseleni River.

Handmade clay pots for sale.

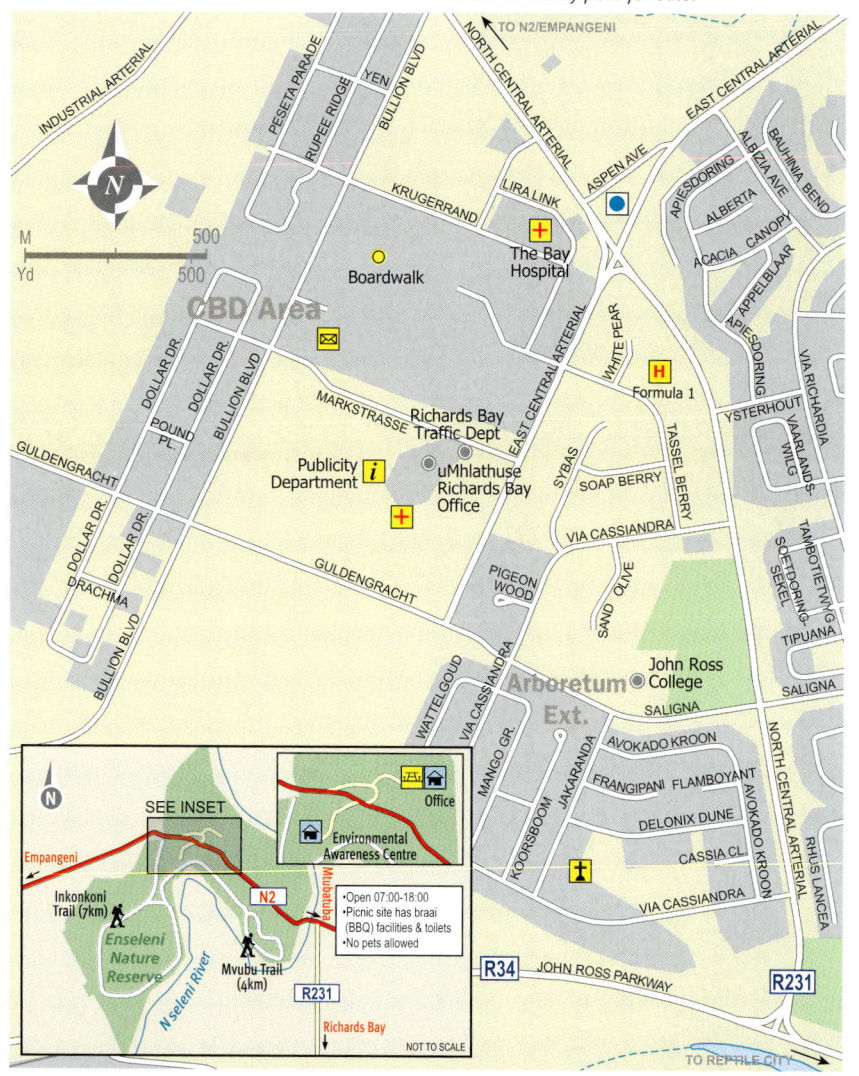

Ulundi was the site of the final acts of the Anglo-Zulu War (in 1879) prior to the region falling under British rule.

Ulundi Ulundi Ulundi Ulundi Ulundi

The heart and capital of the Zulu nation, Ulundi is a charming and heart-warming town which is happy to show-off its heritage: most of the streets in town are named after great Zulu leaders, heroes and personalities. Cetshwayo's father, King Mpande, lies buried in a memorial grave off King Zwelithini Street, while the eMakhosini Valley of the Kings is the traditional burial ground of most of the former Zulu kings. A statue of legendary Zulu leader Shaka stands between the Legislative Assembly and the Government Offices. King Solomon Street is named after the legendary king for whom Rider Haggard published his classic novel King Solomon's Mines in 1885.

Dwellings near Ulundi.

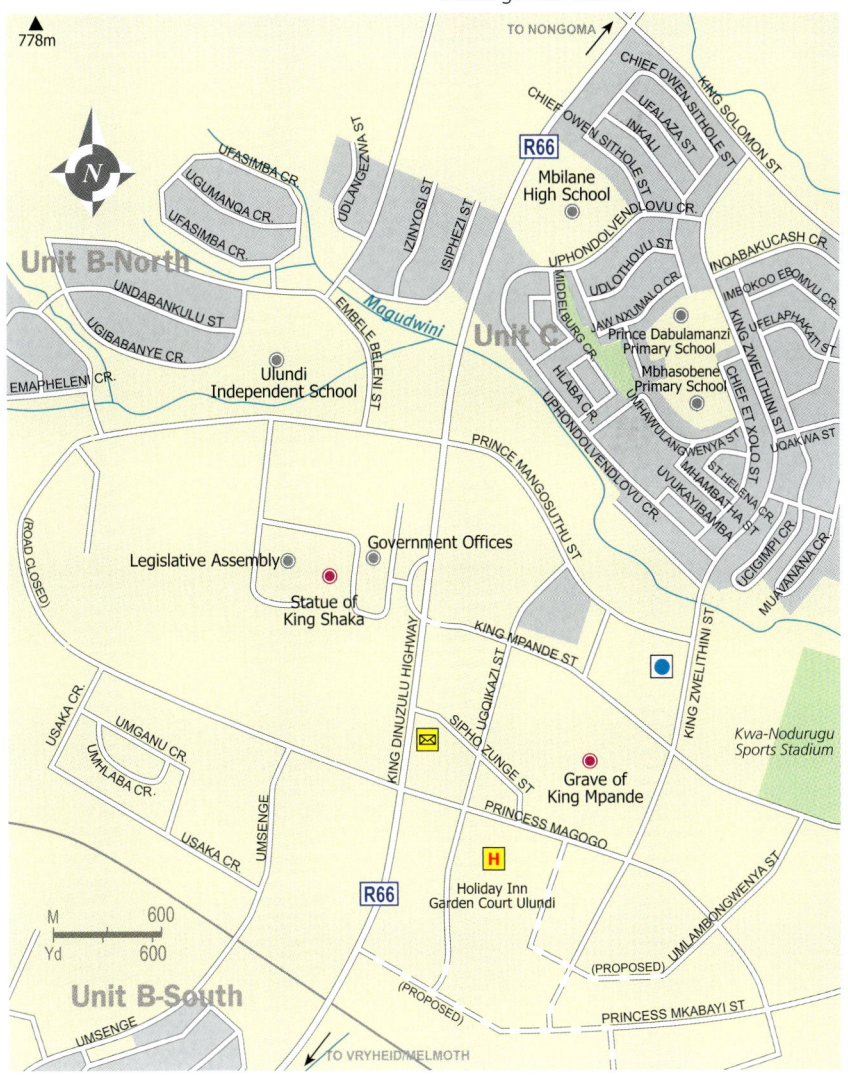

45

Rich in the history of the dominant forces of the province's numerous battles, Melmoth is an important cog in the Zululand birding route.

Melmoth Melmoth Melmoth Melmo

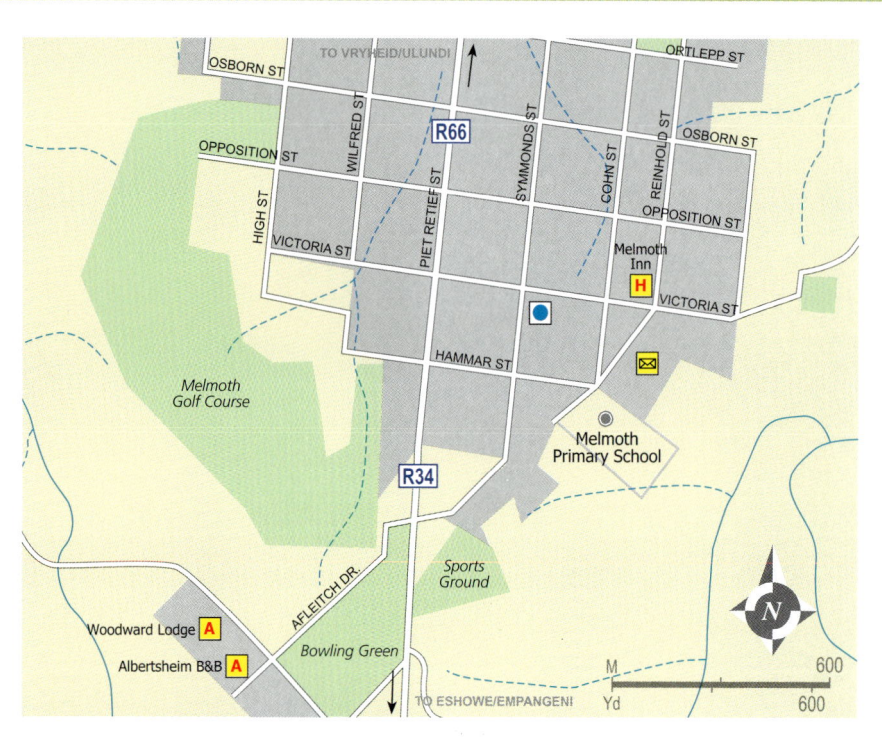

Zulu girl collecting water.

Melmoth is a town based on healthy agricultural production, which befits the pastoral heritage of the nearby tourist tributes to the Zulu nation. Simunye Cultural Village offers a marvelous introduction to the culture and tradition of the Zulu nation, while Shakaland is a grand Zulu-themed park with daily shows that detail Zulu dance as well as tours of the village. Watch traditional spearmaking, Sangoma rituals ... and even a beer ceremony (few guys think of calling it a 'ceremony').

Top Tip

Melmoth has great walks and trails, notably the Kwanzimela Hiking Trail, while the Qwibi Horse Trail gives you a horse's eye-view of the countryside.

46

Crocodiles, snakes and other (mammal!) predators can sometimes be seen lurking around the breeding beaches of the resolute loggerhead turtle.

Zululand's Wildlife Zululand's Wildl

GRAB SHELL, DUDE
The coastal resort town of Cape Vidal in the St Lucia Marine Reserve is right next to the happy breeding ground of a colony of 1000kg-plus giant leatherback turtles. The turtle season is in the South African summer and these 'shelled giants' laboriously swim through the beach sand at night to nest and deposit their eggs – a labour of love they carry out 10 times per season. Hatching happens from February as hundreds of babies struggle through the sand and past predators to sink into the ocean's waves.

BLACK OR WHITE?
The third-largest land mammal, the Black Rhino hold their heads high when walking and expand their feet as each step touches the ground. They create a real commotion when they get an aggressive bee in their bonnet, stomping up dust, slamming their horns against vegetation and letting out shrieks, grunts and snorts while mock-charging. Not a happy camper! The White rhino has a 20cm-wide square lip (black has a pre-hensile upper lip), enlarged neck hump and horns that are less even in size.

A LOAD OF CROC
The dinosaurs' closest living relative, the Nile crocodile can live as long as 100 years and might reach up to 6 metres in length. It also has the most advanced brain of all reptiles. The mother vibrates her body in the water when a predator is around – the 'vibes' are felt by her babies, who dive deep to avoid capture.

FISH EAGLE
The fish eagle – known as the voice of Africa – is not afraid to throw its head back and let out a loud cry, almost like a yelp. This dramatic prince of the African skies utters a drawn-out, lonesome call as it flies gracefully through the air. Fish eagles prey on mice and other birds, but are best known for the dramatic photo opportunities they present when they swoop down on the water's surface to pluck an unsuspecting fish for dinner.

HIPPO ... OR PSYCHO!
Hippos have been the downfall of many a quiz hopeful, as not everyone knows that these chunky, clunky beasts kill more people than any other African mammal. They might chomp the odd boat but, surprisingly, these jittery lugs (weighing in at over a ton) are so scared of having their path to water blocked that they charge over anyone in their path. Talk about paranoid!

Top: *The African Fish Eagle.*
Center: *Rhino.*
Bottom: *Hippopotamus.*

A water wonderland for man and animal, the Greater St Lucia Wetland Park is a world heritage site that covers five eco-systems.

St Lucia Wetland Reserve St Lucia

The St Lucia Wetland Park has been proclaimed a World Heritage Site and includes the St Lucia Game Reserve, False Bay Park, St Lucia Marine Reserve, Sodwana Bay National Park, Maputaland Marine Reserve and Mkuzi Game Reserve. Nature lovers and eco-tourists will find bucketloads with which to amuse and excite themselves in the wetlands. There are mangroves, swamps, lagoons and five eco-systems that form one of the most incredible eco-destinations on earth. They include seashore and dune forest, fresh water lakes, wetlands, mangrove swamps, dry savannah and papyrus banks. Within this 32,800 ha reserve – which includes a coastline stretching alone some 280km – the Greater St Lucia Wetland Park on Lake St Lucia is one of the largest estuaries on the African continent. As well as providing a nursery for innumerable species of marine life it boasts some 1200 crocodiles, 800 hippos and numerous species of bird life, including the famous family of fish eagles.

CAPE VIDAL
The enthusiast can sail, fish, swim and snorkel along this very beautiful stretch of beach with its world-renowned game fishing opportunities. Fishermen have notched up record catches of challenging game like marlin and barracuda. Salt-water fly-fishing addicts will enjoy Mission Rocks in particular.

Top: Loggerhead young, heading for the ocean.
Above: Nile Crocodile with babies.
Below: Cape Vidal.

St Lucia acts as a base to explore the surrounding countryside like no other in the country.

St Lucia Wetland Reserve

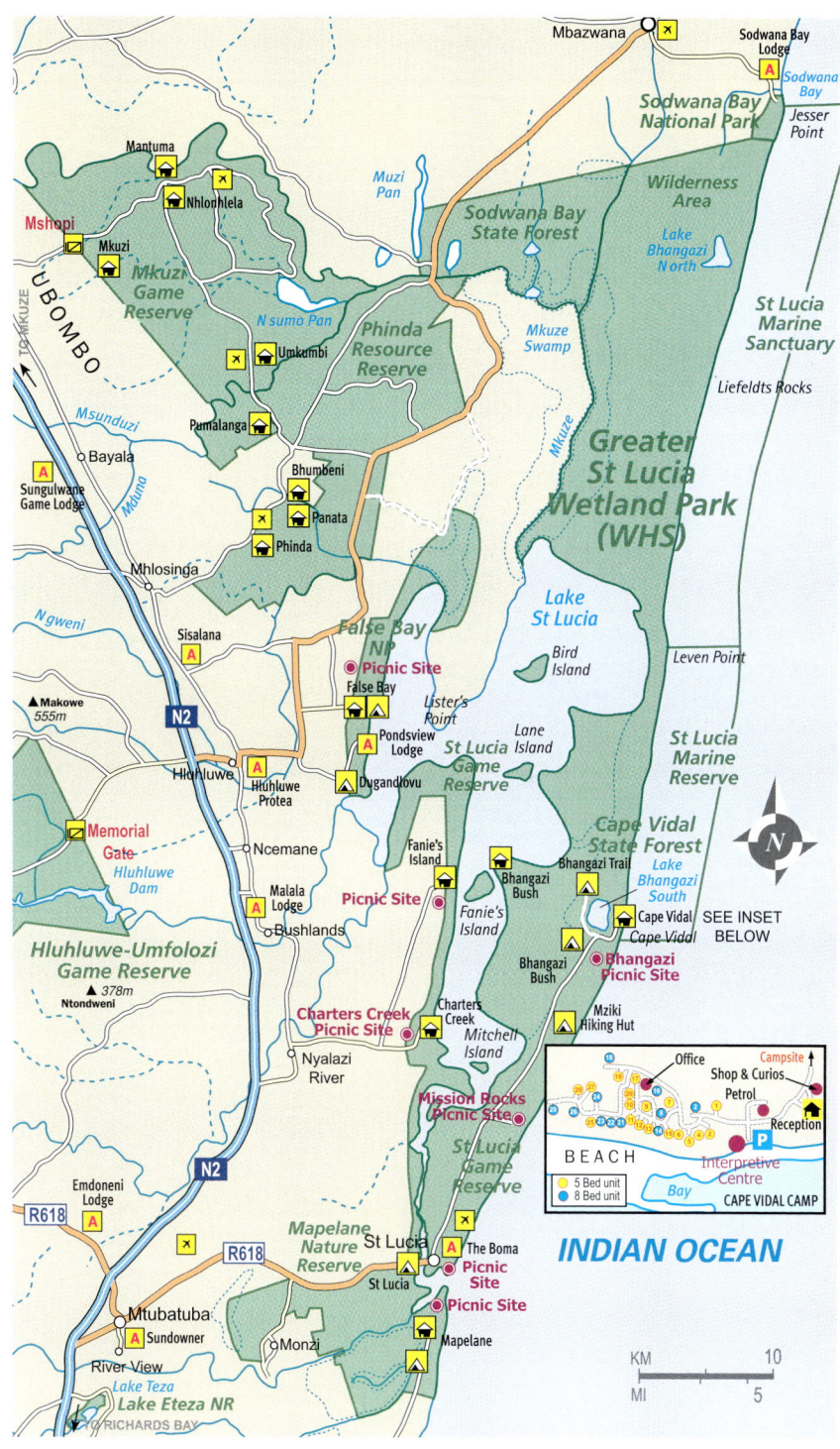

49

Visitors to Hluhluwe-Umfolozi with time on their hands can meet at least a fifth of the world's black and white rhino population ...

Zululand Parks & Reserves

TEMBE NATIONAL PARK
Lying on the border between South Africa and Mozambique, Tembe proclaims itself as the place of wild and untamed Africa. Boasting the world's largest elephants, Tembe offers great viewing for birders, while Tongoland's nearby reefs are appreciated by scuba divers. The reserve protects what remains of the Maputaland elephant population.

HLUHLUWE-UMFOLOZI PARK
Established in 1895, these are Africa's oldest animal sanctuaries and boast the success of the 1960s' Operation Rhino, which saw white rhino captured and relocated to places of safety in South Africa as well as overseas. Hluhluwe-Umfolozi has the Big Five on offer, along with an amazing diversity of wildlife to please the most hardened nature lovers.

MKUZI GAME RESERVE, ZULULAND
Mkuzi is rich in animal life such as rhino, giraffe, zebra, kudu and impala, yet one of its more unique features is a rare forest of giant fig trees that reach up to 25m in height. Nearly 400 species of bird enjoy the varied vegetation, a resource brutally exploited by the excellent bird hide at Nsumo Pan.

PHINDA PRIVATE GAME RESERVE
Phinda is squeezed in between Mkuzi and St Lucia and has seven habitats that cater for the Big Five and 380 bird species.

Top Tip
For an exhilarating walking adventure go on one of Phinda's walking safaris through pristine wilderness: South African wildlife doesn't come better!

Top: Phinda Game Reserve's African interior.
Above: Mkuzi Game Reserve, fig forest walk.
Below: Fever trees along the Nsumo pan at Mkuzi.

> Pongolapoort's elephants enjoy great conservation assistance, with land being made available to them as 'corridors'.

Zululand Parks & Reserves

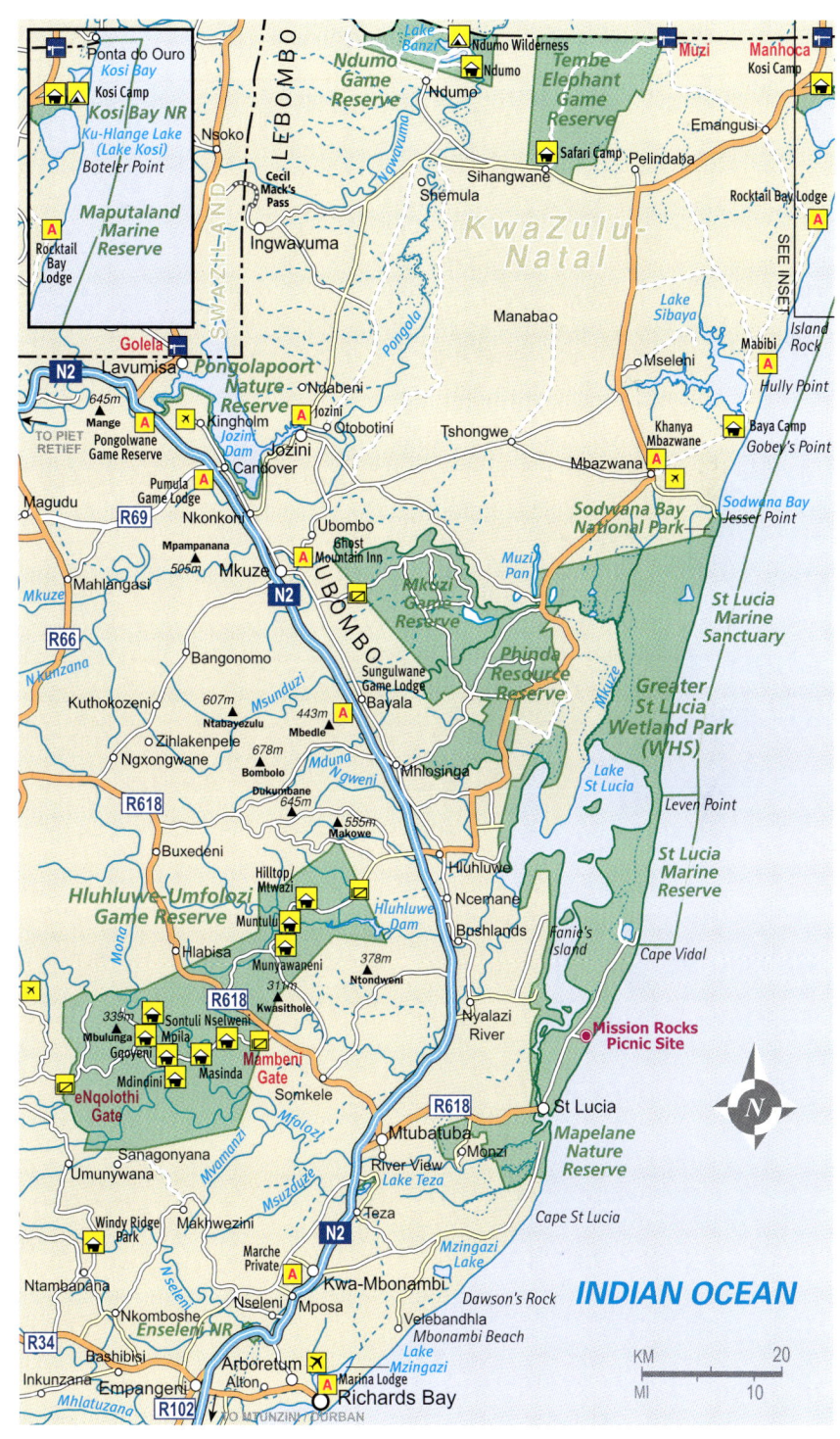

Evidence of fish kraals have been found in other areas to the north of Kosi and as far south as Port St Johns.

St Lucia Sodwana Kosi Bay St Lucia

A fisherman at Kosi Bay using fish traps.

ST LUCIA AND SURROUNDS
Part of the World Heritage Site, St Lucia offers magnificent views from the village, while the Crocodile Centre has a special programme for breeding dwarf and long-snout crocodile (both are endangered species). Around 15km north of St Lucia village there is a much enjoyed braai site at Mission Rock. Staying on the missionary theme, the Grace Mission Station's memory goes way back to the year 1898, and the town has a number of good craft markets to dip into.

KOSI BAY AND SURROUNDS
Exploring Maputaland offers an insight into the Tsonga folk who live in this region. They employ ingenious traditional fish traps positioned close to the mouth of the Kosi Estuary in the splendid eco-system of the Kosi Bay. The famous fish kraals are patrolled by the Tembe and this somewhat primitive (albeit highly-effective) system of catching fish has provided a vital source of sustenance for their people for centuries. This is living history in its most pristine form!

SODWANA BAY
One of the most popular family holiday destinations, Sodwana offers a variety of accommodation ranging from excellent hotels and lodges to self-catering chalets, caravan parks and tent sites. These are located along the many hectares of coastal forest in the area. Fresh produce as well as local craftwork is sold at numerous roadside markets.

Elephant have always migrated between Maputo and Tembe (in SA) elephant reserves along the Futi Channel.

...and continue to..Mozambique

MAPUTO ELEPHANT RESERVE
Lying in the southern-most part of Mozambique, the reserve rests at the meeting point of the rolling hills and the rolling ocean. Prior to the 1975 war there was abundant wildlife in the reserve, but civil war blighted the animal landscape. A great deal of effort has helped to restore some of its faunal heritage, and the park is now proudly decorated by large flocks of flamingoes as well as trumpeting herds of elephant, although their numbers have been reduced to around 400 through the conflict.

INHACA ISLAND
Beautiful tropical beaches and an extensive coral reef ... all just 40km east of Maputo by boat. Inhaca has been largely allocated as a wildlife protection area and has seen many years of scientific research, with abundant specimens on hand such as loggerhead turtles and numerous bird species (pelicans, flamingoes and hammerkops). Worth visiting are the maritime museum and the historic lighthouse, the latter enjoying fantastic snorkelling and diving opportunities, as does the Santa Maria reef.

Top Tip: The 100,000ha Maputo Elephant Reserve offers DIY game drives and bird-watching trips, with guided excursions (and turtle tours!) offered by local camps.
NOTE: a 4x4 vehicle is essential!

Herds of elephant are still seen in Maputo Elephant Reserve.

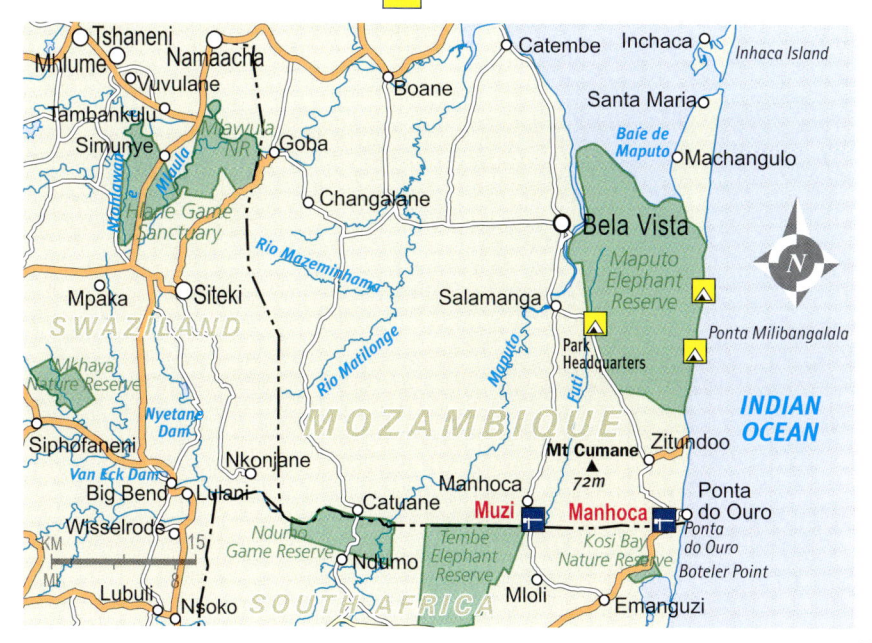

The South Coast is a veritable slice of paradise formerly called Ugu by the region's Zulu ancestors ... meaning Edge of the Great Water.

South Coast South Coast South C

South Coast & Interior

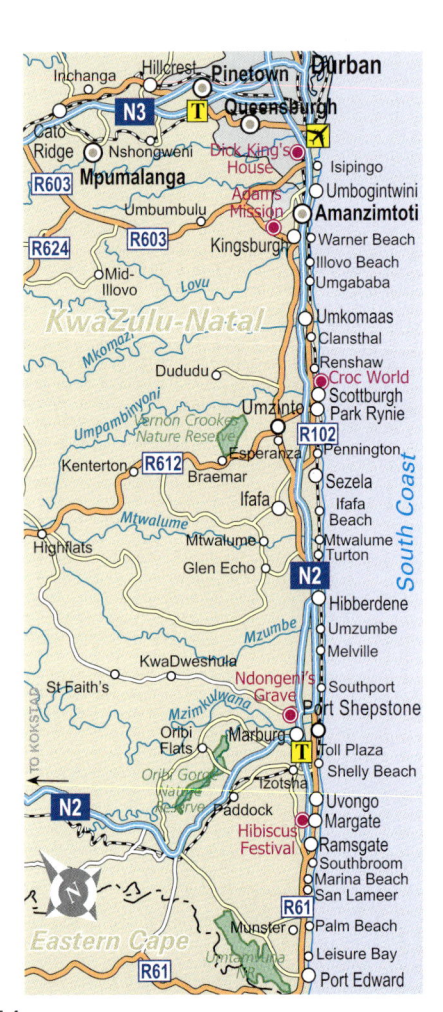

Top: *South coast sunset.*
Above: *Strelitzia, the 'bird of paradise' flower.*

With over a dozen great golf courses along 120km of Indian Ocean Coastline, can you excuse the locals 'fore' calling themselves the Golf Coast! Of course, that does neglect their marvelous beaches with irritating (for eskimoes!) year-round sunshine and unusual tropical bushlands, with whale-watching, hiking, diving, birding, surfing and a wide range of adrenaline and sedate activities on offer. The South Coast might not have it all, but it's as near as dammit! Port Shepstone has the vintage narrow gauge steam train, the Banana Express, for lazy day-trippers, which hints at the enticing interior filled with rolling hills and Zulu folklore. Not for nothing is the South Coast known as one of South Africa's premier holiday spots.

When Shaka tasted the river's water he smiled. "Aaah, the waters are sweet". In Zulu it sounded like "Kanti amanzi mtoti". A river was named!

Amanzimtoti

With glorious, safe beaches, 'Toti is a favourite with sun-worshippers. One of the world's most famous 'messengers', Dick King's old house can now be visited by 'travellers in trouble' – the local traffic department have moved into old Dick's restored homestead. For a bit of an adventure tackle the Ilanda Wilds in Isundu Drive – three trails (Loerie, Mpiti and Mongoose) kick off in town and drift through lush vegetation and along the riverbank. The Amanzimtoti Bird Sanctuary (on Umdoni Road) is open daily and provides a lovely retreat: picnic and feed the wild ducks that float around the small lake. If lakes are your thing, stop in at the Japanese Gardens (Fynn Road): it offers another tranquil setting with a sundeck, birdlife and a miniature lake! The 36ha Umbobavango Nature Reserve also has plenty of birdlife as well as some smaller game.

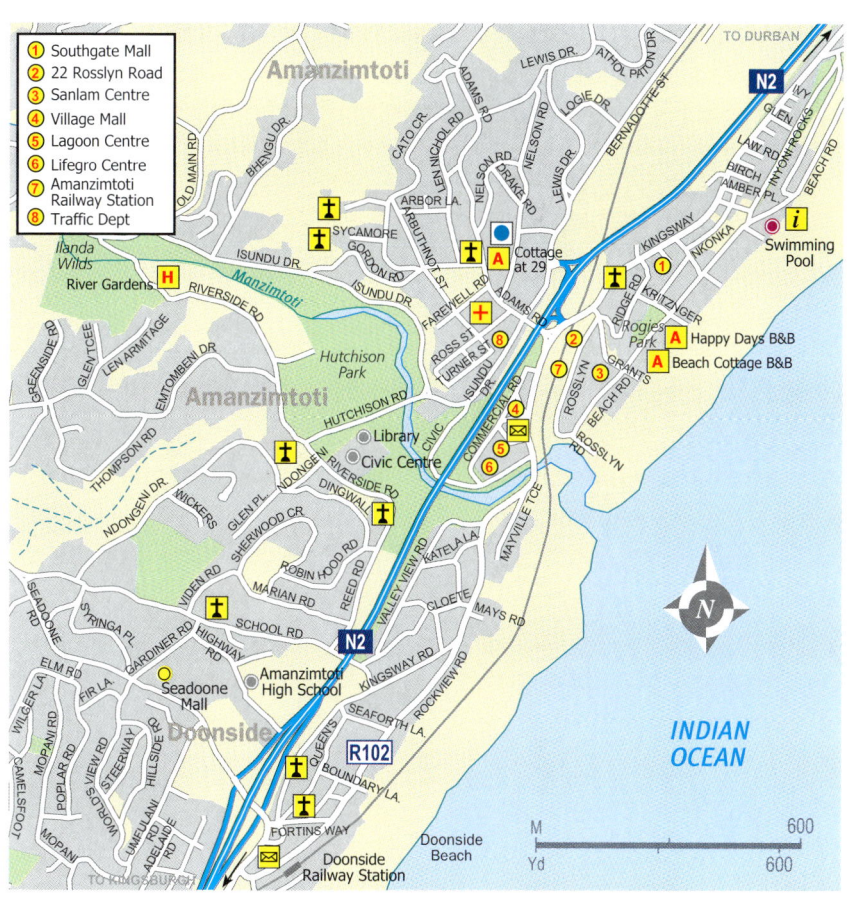

1. Southgate Mall
2. 22 Rosslyn Road
3. Sanlam Centre
4. Village Mall
5. Lagoon Centre
6. Lifegro Centre
7. Amanzimtoti Railway Station
8. Traffic Dept

Kingsburgh is the name given to a number of seaside resort towns ... including the Borough of Kingsburgh. Poor postmen!

Kingsburgh Kingsburgh Kingsburgh

KINGSBURGH
The resorts in the Kingsburgh coastal stretch – just past popular Amanzimtoti, and not far from Durban – are made up of Warner Beach, St Winifred's Beach / Doonside Beach, Winklespruit, Illovo Beach and Karridene. These 'hamlets' are all popular thanks to their proximity to Durban ... not to mention for offering languid lagoons and wide, rolling beaches with shark-net protected 'safe' swimming. Ski-boaters and surfers will also 'weigh anchor' with glee here along the almost 10km stretch of white sand coastline.

VERNON CROOKES NATURE RESERVE
Lying inland from Scottsburgh, Vernon Crookes Nature Reserve rambles over 2000 hectares of hilly landscape and is home to almost 100 species of mammals, fish, amphibians and reptiles, as well as more than 300 types of bird. Night drives, 12km of tourist roads, accommodation and a lovely picnic site complete the picture of an enjoyable (and highly accessible) wildlife experience.

> **Top Tip**
> Be sure to use insect repellents in Vernon Crookes NR, especially on the short trails: ticks are a problem in the area.

Scottburgh's Surf Lifesaving Club has notched up over 5000 rescues since its first patrol in 1929.

Scottburgh

An easy drive from Durban, Scottburgh offers the best in local beaches, forests and surrounding hillsides. The town's fine stretch of golden beach (and its popular lagoon) are major tourist magnets: water enthusiasts can swim, canoe, sunbathe or ride the supertube. Nearby Crocworld offers an incredible wildlife experience as you walk within biting distance of these prehistoric monsters ... yet enjoy perfect safety. There are many other attractions also aside from the 10,000 crocs! The 60ha **TC ROBERTSON NATURE RESERVE** on the outskirts of town boasts over 200 bird species and plenty of other wildlife to enjoy along the many trails.

Spot the Grey Heron in the TC Robertson reserve!

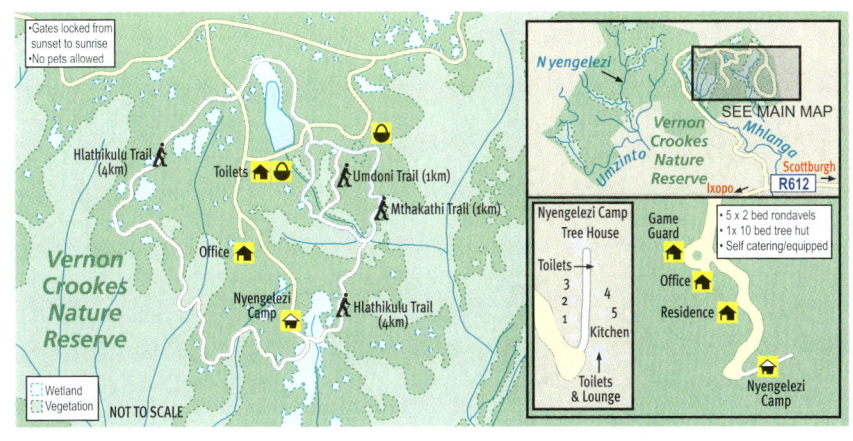

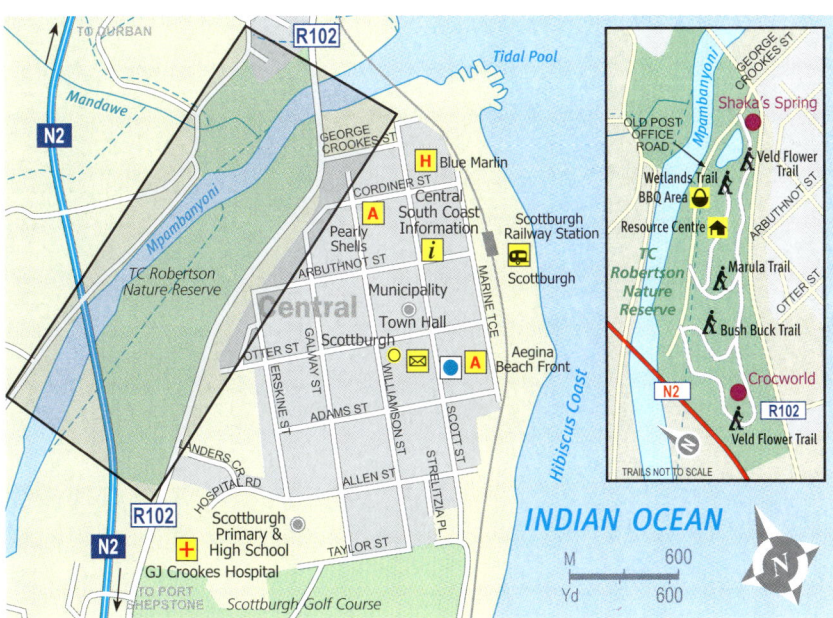

57

A delight of a resort town, Hibberdene is the halfway point between Durban and Port Edward, and a good spot to cast a fishing line.

Hibberdene Port Shepstone Hibbe

PORT SHEPSTONE

KZN's largest South Coast town boasts one of SA's premier golf courses (the river-flanked Port Shepstone CC), the maritime-themed Port Shepstone Museum, fine beaches and tidal pools. The famous Banana Express (see page 13) kicks off in town, winding passengers through plantations of bananas and sugarcane up to Oribi Gorge (stopping for a gorgeous stroll). The black and white lighthouse was built in Scottburgh in 1906 but was moved to Port Shepstone a year later!

HIBBERDENE

If Hibberdene's great beaches and fishing aren't enough, look out for Fish Eagles further down the Mzimayi River, or go quad biking with the staff of Mzimayi River Lodge.

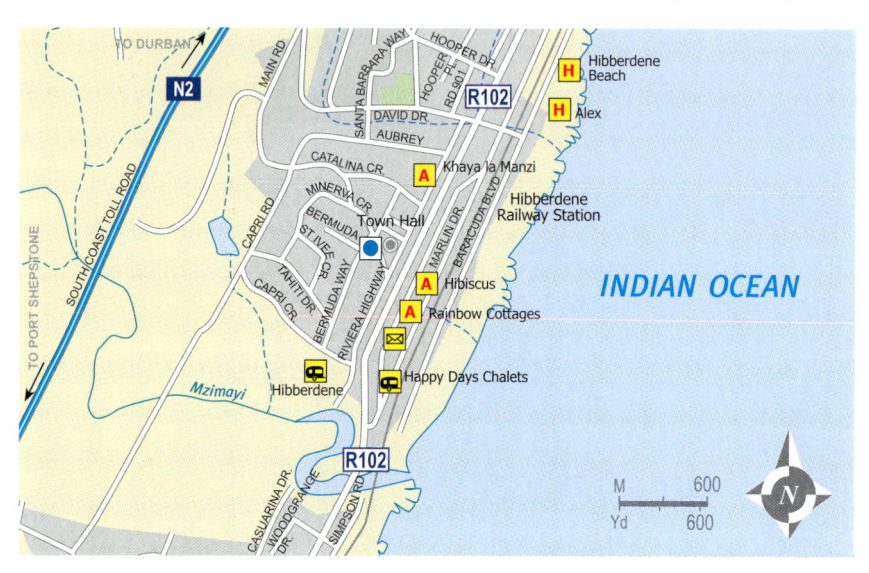

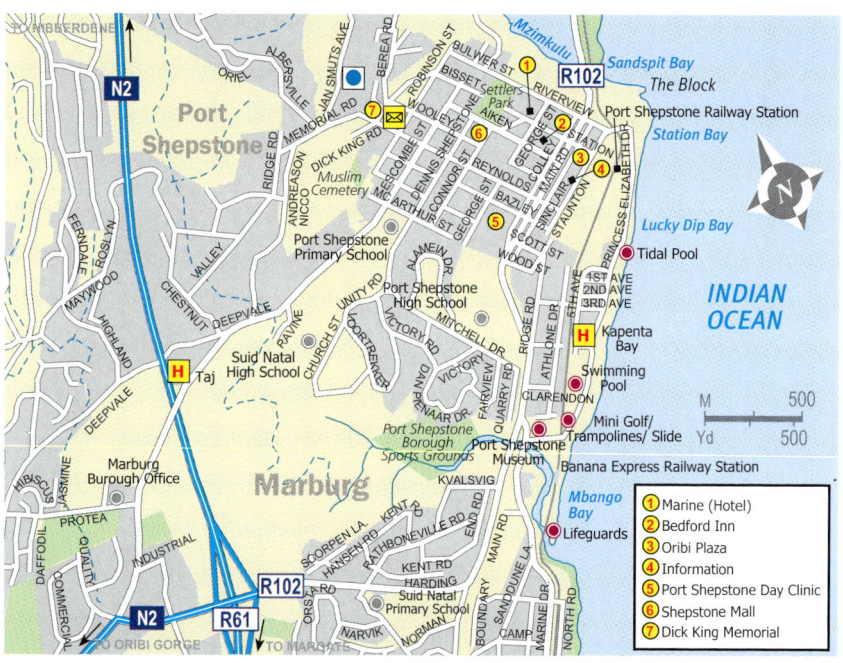

58

The Oribi Gorge's beauty and tranquility is a great stress-reliever ... while its adrenaline jaunts are a great stress-creator!

Oribi Gorge

Just over 20km inland from Port Shepstone, the Umzimkhulu River carved the astounding Oribi Gorge through the local terrain: 24km long, 5km wide and 300m deep. There are scores of super riverside picnic spots and a host of great walks and trails (including horseback trails) through the reserve packed with birdlife (over 250 species). The gorge is not a good place for the faint-hearted to lose a beat: adventure activities include 'wild' mountain-biking, a 110m abseil, wild water rafting (grade 3+ rapids), a 120m-long Gorge Slide (a foofy-slide starting 170m high) and a terrifying Gorge Swing (freefall 70m before hurtling across the gorge in a 100m arc ... so leave the breakfast table early!).

The Gorge's gorgeous views.

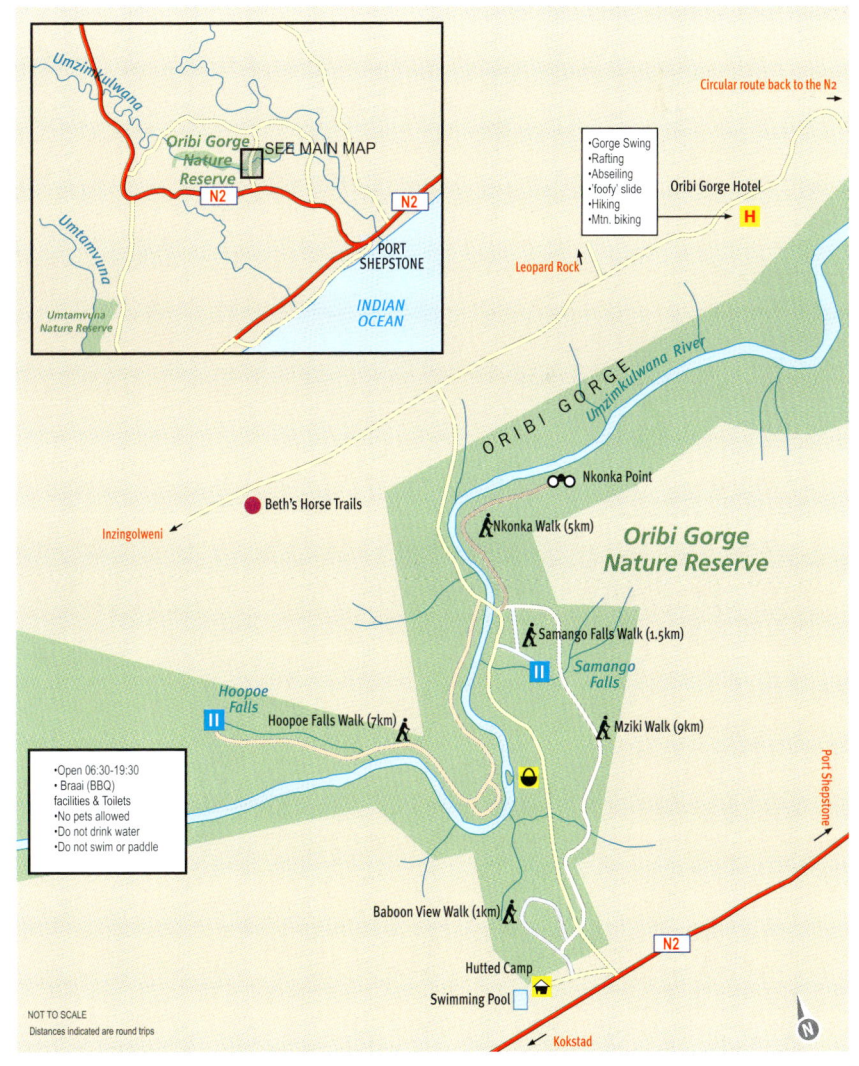

- Open 06:30-19:30
- Braai (BBQ) facilities & Toilets
- No pets allowed
- Do not drink water
- Do not swim or paddle

NOT TO SCALE
Distances indicated are round trips

From its heady days as an isolated, palm-fringed beach, Margate has grown into a slick holiday haven with its own municipal airport.

Margate Margate Margate Margate

Lucienne point, Margate.

Quite the place for the socially active, and Margate boasts all sorts of accommodation, tourist activities and distractions. If you're bored of Margate then ... well, you're probably just spoilt. Hire a paddle boat, or sit in more relaxed fashion and enjoy a demonstration of the ancient art of basket-weaving.

Stay in touch with Hollywood at the local cinema or enjoy many arts and crafts attractions. The Margate Bird Park might not rival Umgeni, but it's good for the whole family, as is Old Macdonald's Family Farm and the Riverbend Croc Farm (200 smiling Nile crocs) and art gallery.

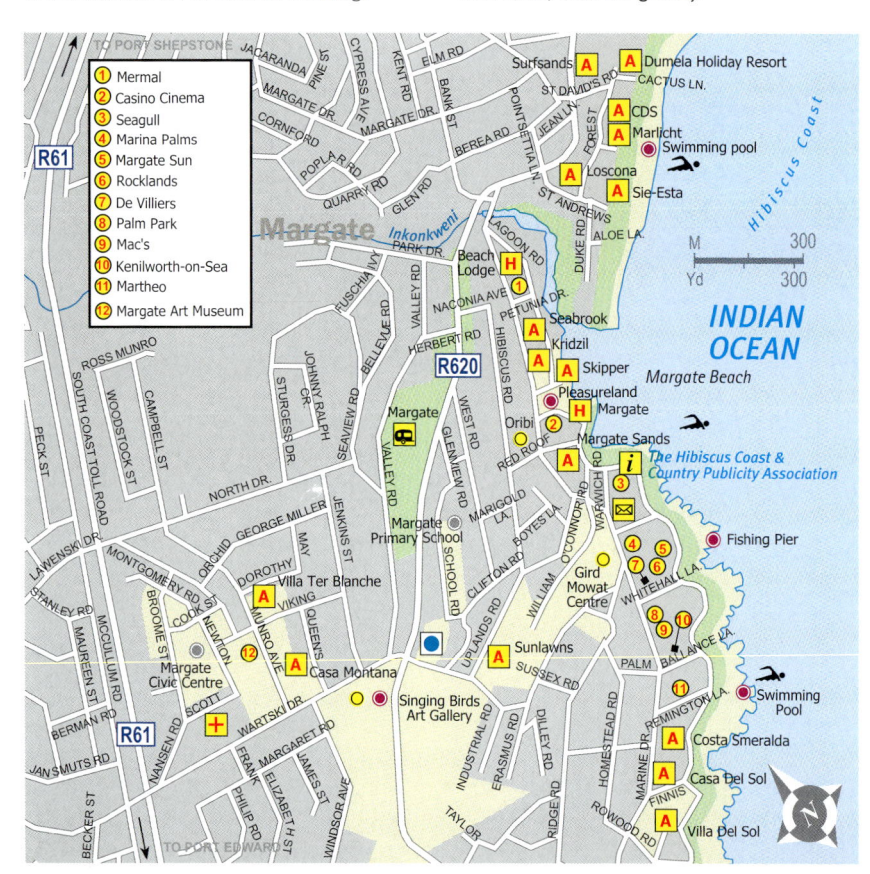

1. Mermal
2. Casino Cinema
3. Seagull
4. Marina Palms
5. Margate Sun
6. Rocklands
7. De Villiers
8. Palm Park
9. Mac's
10. Kenilworth-on-Sea
11. Marthei
12. Margate Art Museum

60

Uvongo's name is a Colonial extraction of the Zulu word iVungu, which describes the roaring waterfall on the Uvongo River.

Uvongo Uvongo River Nature Reserve

Uvongo is a tremendously popular spot on the KZN South Coast and yet another gorgeous coastal resort ... but with a difference. Not only does a river run through it, but a whole nature reserve runs through, even with a hippo pool. The reserve includes a 23m waterfall, rapids and some good hiking trails (including a two-hour circular walk) through the coastal forest. The fauna is a diverse array of orchids, ferns, shrubs and trees, all inhabited by a wide range of coastal birds. The town lies just over 10km from Port Shepstone and rests on cliffs overlooking the ocean and a shark net-protected beach popular with swimmers and surfers. Uvongo is made up of St Michael's-on-Sea, Uvongo Beach and Manaba Beach townships. Between St. Michael's-on-Sea and Uvongo Beach are the famous rocks – Pothole and Orange – which offer great fishing yields, although the pier on the the south side of Uvongo Beach also lures fishermen in.

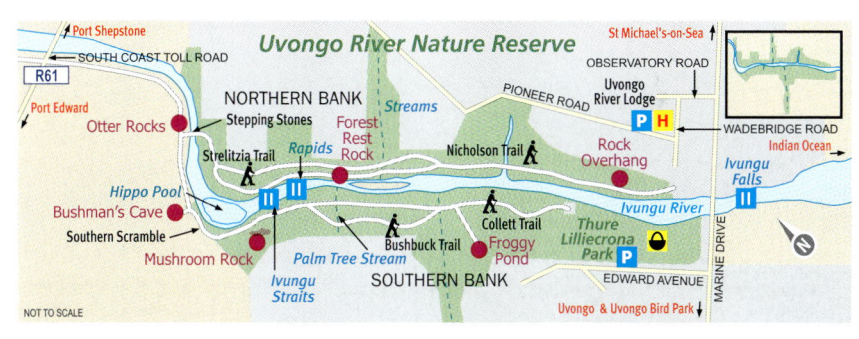

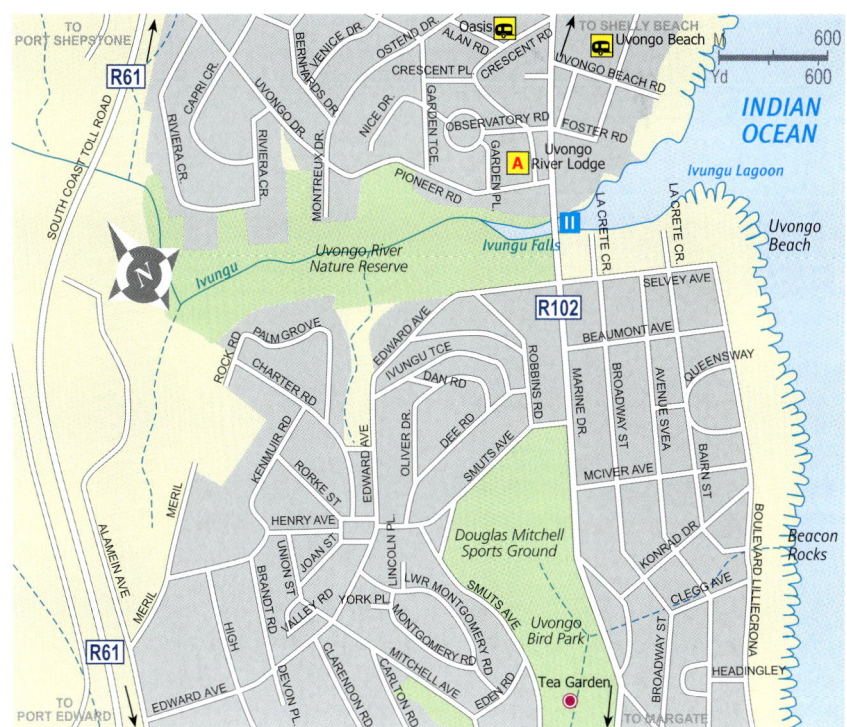

> **Top Tip**
> Uvongo's famous 23m waterfall empties into one of South Africa's deepest lagoons. The town has tidal, paddling and natural rock pools for kids to explore.

61

Ramsgate sits above some of the warm Indian Ocean coast's finest beaches, protected by shark nets and ever-present lifeguards.

Ramsgate

RAMSGATE
Choose from plenty of bays, beaches, a tidal pool and a lagoon that offer plenty of holiday options and act as a welcome buffer to the north wind. Just 2km 'down the drag' from Margate, Ramsgate is considered a suburb of the former.

UMTAMVUNA NATURE RESERVE
This most southerly of KZN's reserves runs along 19km of the Umtamvuna River. Relatively quiet, the hiking trails will reward you with dramatic landscapes, fabulous fauna, eagle-eyed Cape Vultures and thick rainforests in a sandstone-walled gorge.

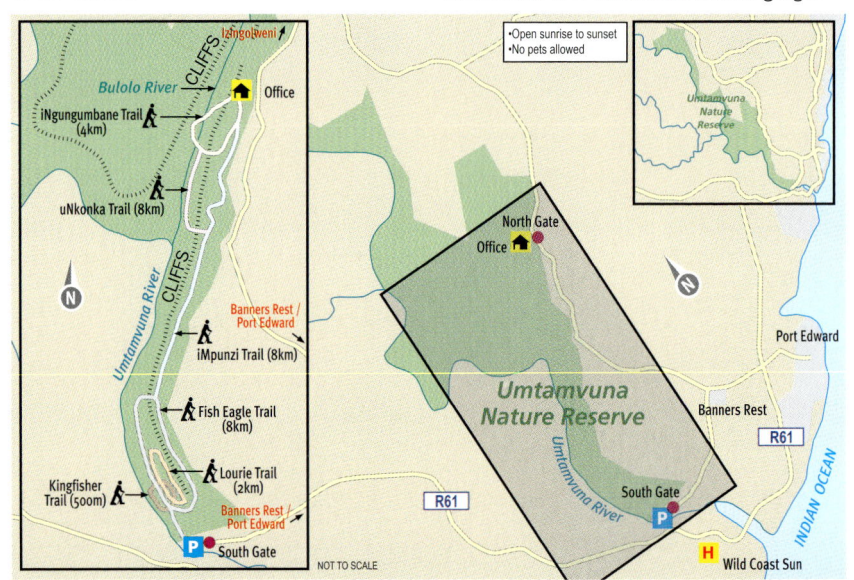

The town was named in honour of the future King Edward, and its history is littered with settlers, sailors ... and shipwrecks.

Port Edward

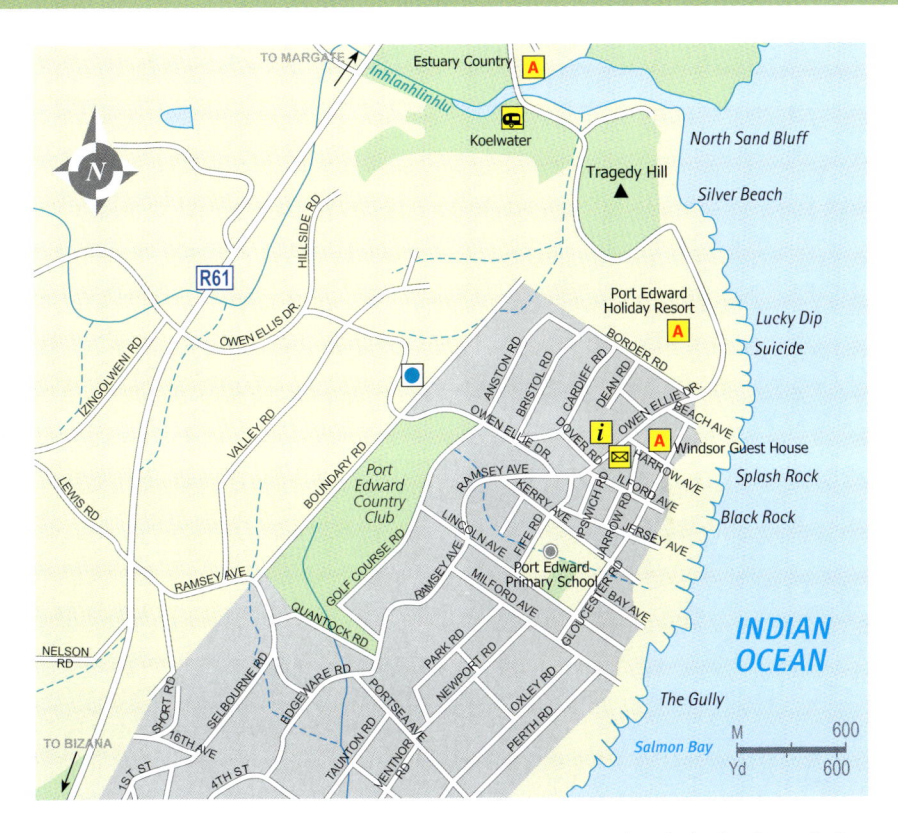

An ideal base for anyone visiting the little-known Umtamvuna Nature Reserve as well as the nearby African Mzamba Village, a Xhosa village-inspired theme park. The coastline is littered with stunning beaches, and a 9-hole golf course with great sea views, as well as tennis and squash, make it a fun destination.

Other sites to visit include the dramatic Port Edward bridge over the Umtamvuna River (and into the Eastern Cape), as well as the historic Tragedy Hill, which overlooks Silver Beach. It was here that (according to legend) early trader Henry Fynn and his family were killed in error by Zulus who thought they had stolen their cattle.

Bottlenose Dolphins and a whale playing in the surf around Port Edward.

63

A thriving rural community whose history is linked up with the Griqua people and their famed leader, Adam Kok.

Kokstad Mount Currie Nature Reserv

Sunflower on a clear, blue Kokstad day.

Adam Kok (the third!) gave the town its name over a century ago … and he and his wife were laid to rest in a mausoleum on the main street, while a bust of this brave Griqua leader stands in the town centre. A delightful museum in the former library and highlights the Griqua people's history as well as Kokstad's military past. There are exciting options for adrenaline junkies (such as paragliding and other sports) around Kokstad and in nearby East Griqualand towns. Horse riding, and especially polo playing, is a popular pastime in town, and the Kokstad Polo Club is well-renowned.

MOUNT CURRIE NATURE RESERVE

This beautiful reserve was named after Sir Walter Currie, a police commander and a fervent champion of the Griqua people. Bird-watchers and lovers of the outdoors will enjoy the Crystal Springs Dam and the 1700ha Mount Currie reserve will delight the visitor who has more than half an eye on boating, fishing or nature trails. Of historical interest is a WWI Memorial, a Monument at Adam Kok's encampment site as well as an historic Griqua Cemetery.

> **Top Tip**
> Kokstad's 18-hole golf course will test even the best of handicaps, while flyfishing in the well-stocked dams and rivers around town is a pleasure.

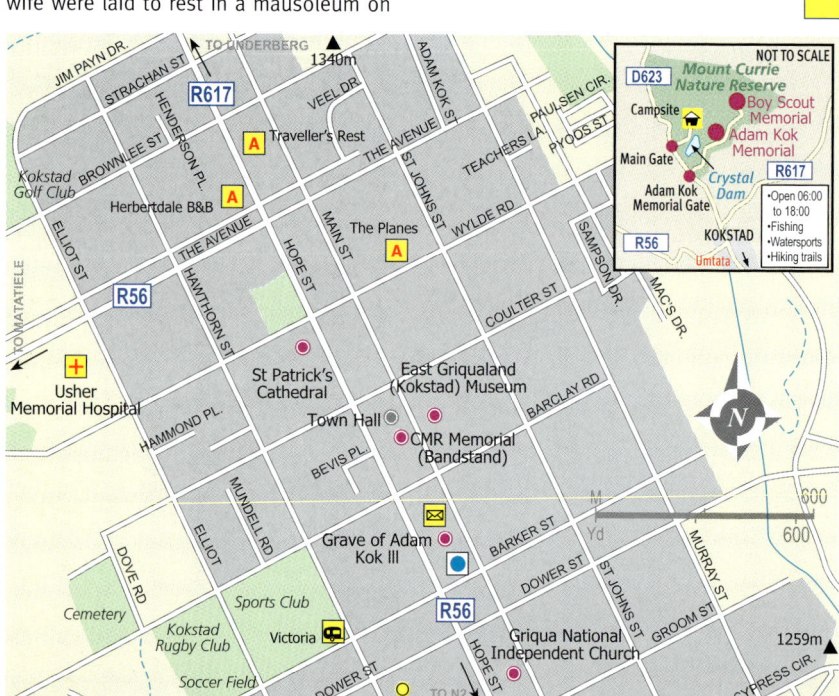

"There is a lovely road which runs from Ixopo into the hills. These hills are grass covered and rolling, they are lovely, beyond any singing of it." – Alan Paton

Route 617

IXOPO
Ixopo is a delightful Zulu town resting in its majestic midlands countryside, and it draws its name from a Zulu onomatopoeia that describes the squelching sound made by a herd of cattle wading through a muddy field. The historic Agricultural Hall (a charming building which has earned national monument status for itself!) is now home to a bank. For the forensically inclined the Dead Man's Tree is a must see: found just outside the old Post Office building, the tree used to serve as a notice board for announcements of deaths and funerals.

UNDERBERG
Underberg is a mountain hideaway on the Sani Saunter range near the bottom reaches of the Drakensberg, a little over 40km by road to the Park's border. It lies at the foot of the famous Sani Pass. Himeville is a shade over 5km away, with a dozen B&B establishments located around Underberg, plus a good few airfields. The town is an hour and a half's drive from Pietermaritzburg and an hour from Kokstad. An excellent base for exploring the 'Berg or engaging in fishing trips, this beautiful area just happens to be packed with trout dams and natural trout-rich streams. Animosity between Himeville and Underberg was laid to rest in 1970 when a row of oak trees was planted between the settlements. The town is involved with Splashy Fen and the alternative-lifestyle supporters it attracts every year.

SANI SAUNTER
A trip along the Sani Saunter is a specific delight for the arts and crafts crew, although there is a wide range of goods on display to suit many tastes. The San people once populated this area in large numbers, and their memory lives on in the saunter's name.

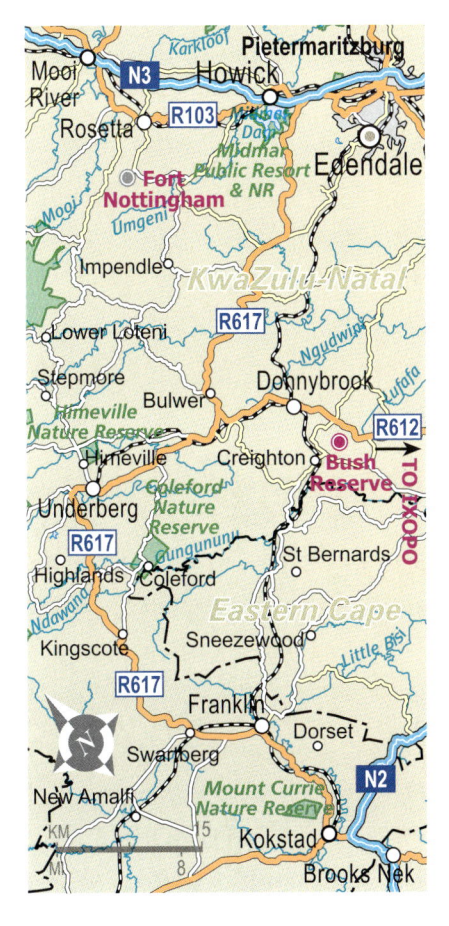

Sani Pass.

The famous Midlands Meander is a unique mix of more than 160 places to eat, drink, sleep, shop, play and generally have fun.

Kloof to Mooi River

Kloof to Pietermaritzburg to Mooi River

Visit the Valley of 1000 Hills.

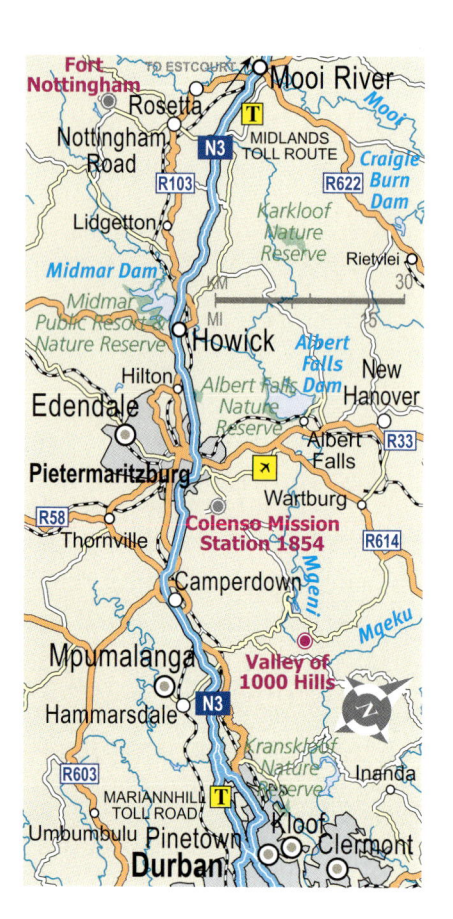

This area is a paradise for visitors fascinated by craftwork, arts, top class restaurants as well as offering a huge variety of sporting, environmental and historical opportunities. Visitors are enticed to explore the galleries and studios of artists and crafters, resulting in the Midlands Meander growing into a varied and fascinating journey into the world of its arts and crafts. Exercise and the pursuit of sport, enrichment of the mind and visual delights abound in this area ... although the visitor is advised (nay, encouraged!) to linger and enjoy its many delights in as unhurried a fashioned as dictated by the local towns and villages and their people. Oops, I think I left my watch at home ...

Rawdons Hotel.

Legend has it that the famous American writer Mark Twain named the valley during his visit at the end of the 19th century.

Valley of 1000 Hills

Local boys in the valley.

This valley is breathtakingly beautiful and one can almost feel the special historical importance of the area and the wandering spirits of 'the ancestors'. Across the rolling hills can be seen Inanda Dam, situated on the Mgeni River: countless early Iron Age settlement sites have been uncovered here. The world-famous Duzi Canoe Marathon entices canoeists from around South Africa to take part in this gruelling race every January. The small village of Drummond is the halfway point of one of the toughest road races in the world, the Comrades' Marathon, a race that attracts runners from all around the world … to the pained amusement of millions of TV viewers.

THE SHONGWENI SHUFFLE
Shongweni boasts some incredible sandstone formations, lush forests and a wide range of game. Its name comes from the Zulu word Ntshonweni (column of smoke), after the spray from the waterfall on the Ugede River. The Shongweni Shuffle commences along Kassier Road and crosses the N3, then forks to Shongweni Village on the T5 and then on to the Shongweni Dam on the T6.

Top Tip
At the village of Monteseel visitors can steal a look at one of the oldest Cycads in the world.

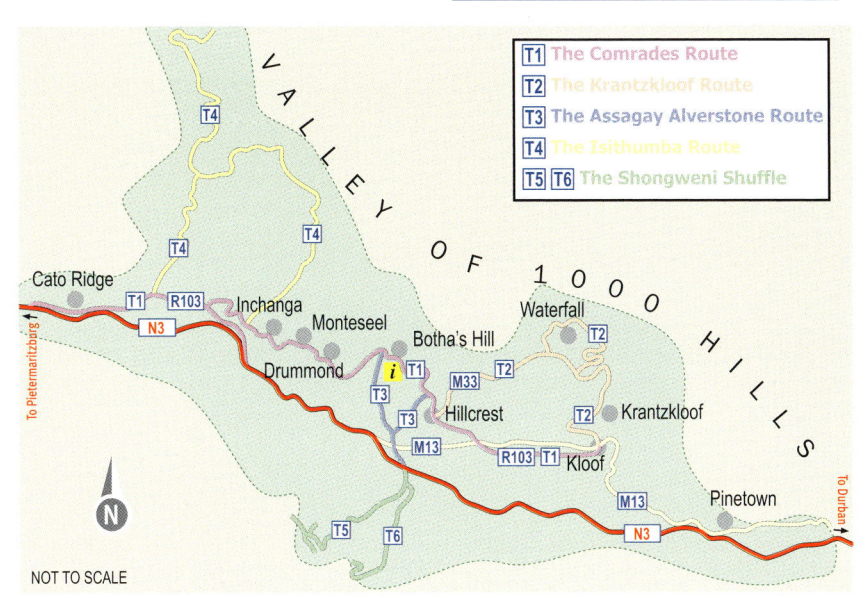

- T1 The Comrades Route
- T2 The Krantzkloof Route
- T3 The Assagay Alverstone Route
- T4 The Isithumba Route
- T5 T6 The Shongweni Shuffle

67

KZN's capital is named after two of the all-time great Voortrekker leaders: Piet Retief and Gerrit Maritz.

Pietermaritzburg

A magnificent town to walk around, and boasting some stunning Colonial architecture, Pietermaritzburg is a highly historic town. The user-friendly Natal Museum is one of South Africa's five national museums, while Comrades Marathon House is an archive of one of the world's great road races. The Gandhi Monument commemorates the great social leader's time in South Africa (and the racial incidents that spurred him on the road to his heroic humanitarian cause). The Garden of Remembrance commemorates the South African lives lost in the two World Wars ... while the 'weeping cross' is said to symbolically ooze sap in memory of the horrors of Delville Wood.

Top Tip

Founded in 1870, the charming National Botanical Gardens includes a feature display of a fig tree that stands almost 50m tall.

Queen Victoria statue in front of the old provincial council buildings.

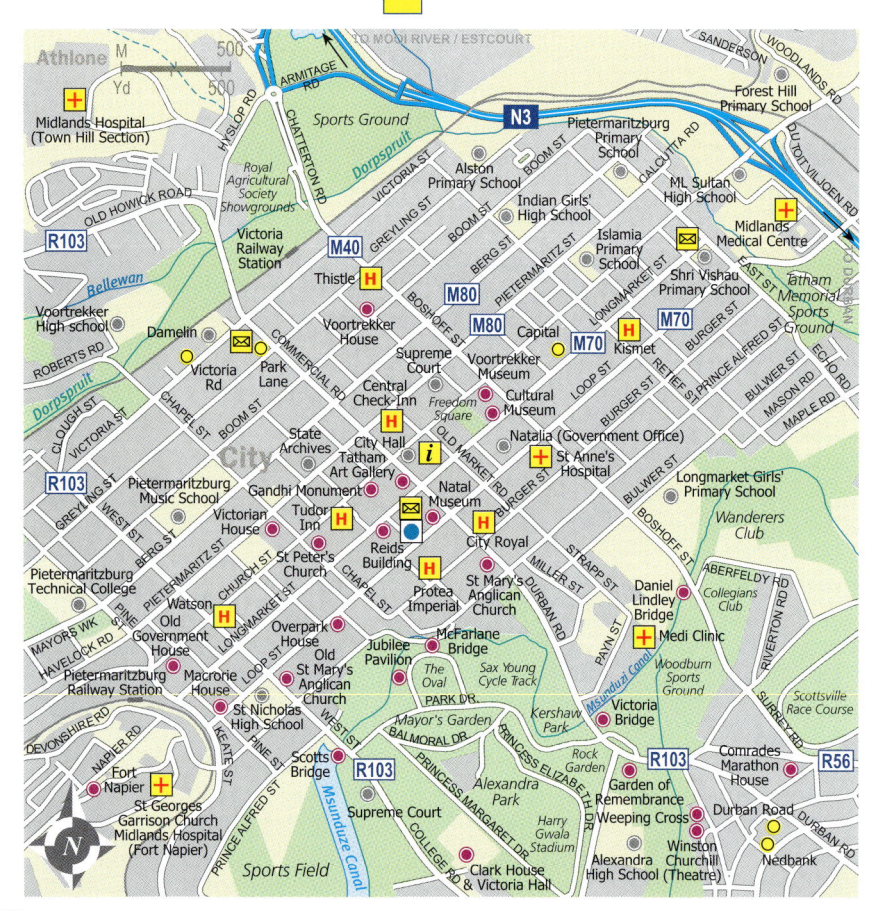

68

The Midmar Dam hosts the annual Midmar Mile swim, 10,000 people taking to the water in the world's largest inland swimming race.

Howick Midmar Howick Midmar

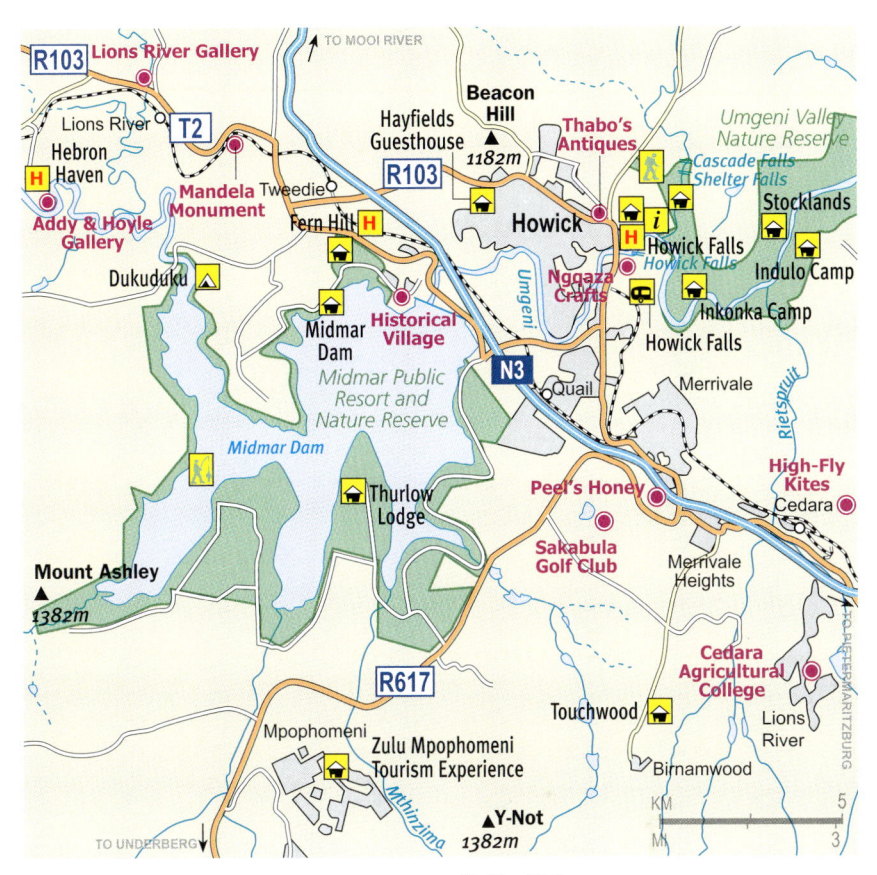

Karkloof falls.

Around 20km north-west of Pietermaritzburg is an amazing area of waterfalls and waterways, with the lovely town of Howick at its centre. There are a number of great hiking trails for visitors to enjoy, while at the same time showing off the beauty and fabulous natural surrounds. Some of the more popular include the historic Howick Town Trail, as well as the Beacon Hill Trail, Umgeni River Trail and the Howick Gorge and Howick Falls trails. Just out of town are the Karkloof Falls, the Cascade Falls and Shelter Falls, as well as the Umgeni Valley Nature Reserve, not to mention a good many campsites. There are plenty of craft diversions a short drive out of town, as well as the Sakabula Golf Club and the Zulu Mpophomeni Tourism Experience. The Midmar Dam is part of the Midmar Public Resort and Nature Reserve, with attractions such as fun rides (on trains and tug boats), picnics, watersports, curios for sale and plenty of enjoyable drives around the reserve. There are also numerous historical and educational exhibits, including the Historical Village and an open-air museum.

69

A national monument, the spectacular Howick Falls send water plunging from around 100m high down into the Umgeni Gorge.

Howick Howick Howick Howick H

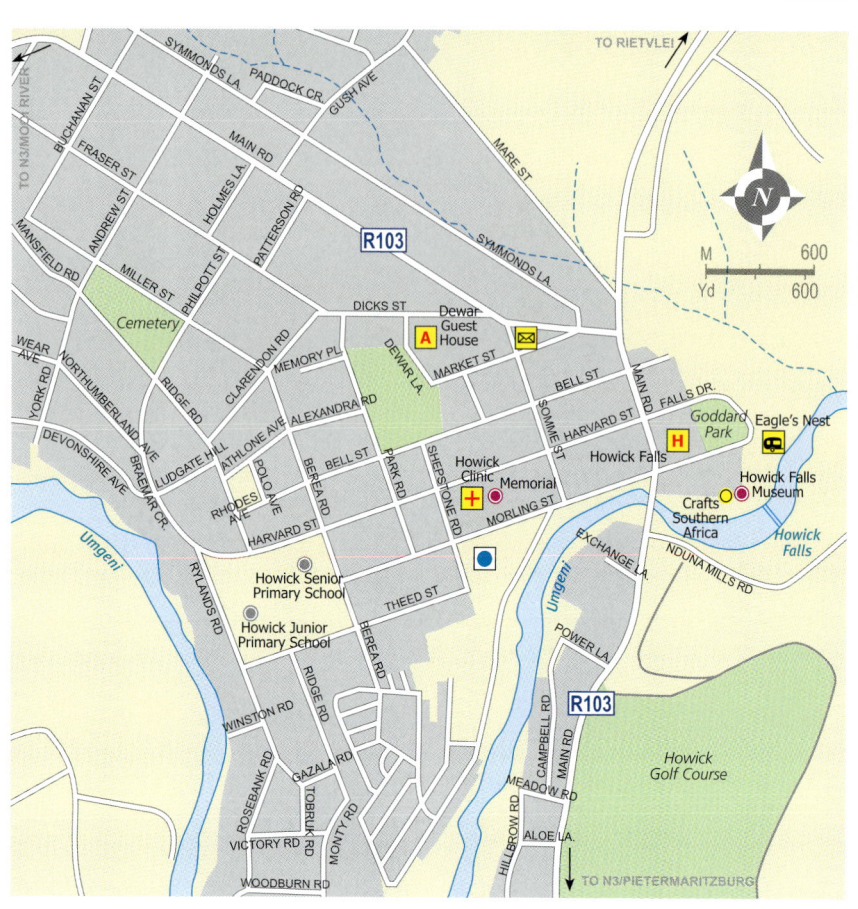

The Umgeni steam train enters Howick station.

The Howick Falls on the edge of town is the focus of a number of great hikes and trails which lead the brave right to the foot of the falls (the brave should not be stupid, as the rocks are extremely slippery: wear appropriate shoes and walk with care). The REALLY brave ... well, they'll take advantage of one of the falls' fresh attractions ... abseiling down 100m! Howick is another big crafts centre, with Crafts Southern Africa being located in the town's former Agricultural Hall. The Howick Museum covers the whole Lions River district and has fascinating period costumes. The Laager Wall isn't a pub ... it's a well-preserved wall dating back to 1879: it was built to hold back the invading Zulus following the ferocious Battle of Isandlwana.

Top Tip
The Zulus know the Howick Falls as kwaNogqaza – in their tongue this describes 'the place of the tall one'.

The Wartburger Inn offers a step to the left and into time-warp territory: traditional fare, teutonic hospitality set in a slice of colonial-styled Germany.

Albert Falls

ALBERT FALLS

For those with a head for heights a walk on the suspension bridge across the Umgeni River will yield rich visual reward, and when you arrive at the falls (where settlers once panned for alluvial gold) there are various species of game to be seen. The Albert Falls Dam, surrounded by a reserve, is a glorious spot for bird-watching and enjoying nature, as well as being great for picnics.

WARTBURG

A merging of German country charm and African rural scenery make a visit to Wartburg an interesting experience. The town has a strong German cultural history which is the seat of much local pride and highlights South Africa's many diverse cultures. Arts and crafts outlets are plentiful and of special interest are hand-painted porcelain and handcrafted woodwork ... not to mention the ancient art of calligraphy.

You'll find great fishing spots around Albert Falls.

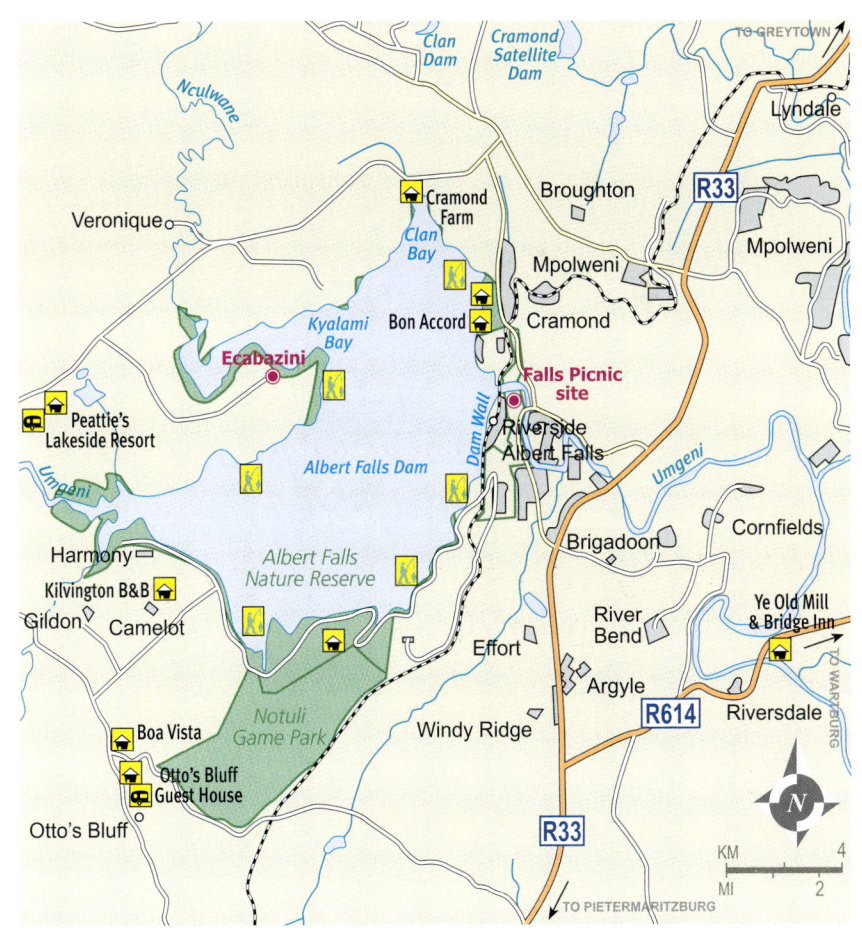

71

An experience to change your life ... and your lifestyle. That's their marketing claims ... and their rate of success is similar to the Trevi Fountain!

Midlands Meander

Bored? No chance if you indulge in the Midlands Meander, which offers so much for visitors to discover in an ever-changing artistic, social and cultural environment. The dramatic Drakensberg mountains, peaceful little country towns, farmland, indigenous forests, the vast waters of the Midmar Dam as well as sparkling little streams. Each season brings changes to tempt the visitor to return again and again, each time to drift through a new route, meet new people and discover new natural and social treaures. Just remember to take your time ... there's no rush, really!

Midlands reservations 033 266 6950
(fax 033 266 6979)
info@midlandsreservations.co.za

Midlands Meander Tourism Association
033 330 8195

A local lady from the Notting Hill area.

PLACES TO STAY IN THE MIDLANDS
Abberley Guest House 033 234 4163
Aird Country House 033 234 4482
Barland B/B 033 234 4293 / 4040
Barretts Country House 033 234 4752
Bellavista Forest Lodge 033 234 4633
Bellwood Cottages 033 266 6218
Cranford Country Lodge 033 330 2182
Dargle Cottages 033 234 4467
Dunroamin Country Guest House
033 263 2045
Everglades Hotel 033 234 4233 / 9001
Features of Fordoun 033 263 6217
Fern Hill Hotel 033 330 5071
FourSprings B/B 033 234 4525
Gleneagles Guesthouse 033 263 2883 B/B
Granny Mouse Country House 033 234 4071
Greenfields Manor House 033 263 1301
Günther's B/B 033 234 4171
Halls Country House 033 263 26 96
Happy Hill Guesthouse 033 234 4380
Hawklee Country house 033 266 6008
Hawkston Farm B/B 033 266 6392
Hebron Haven Family Hotel 033 234 4431
Impafana cottages 033 234 4471
Lythwood Lodge 033 234 4666
Midmar Dam 033 330 2067
Misty Mountain B/B 033 266 6250
Mountain View Country House 033 267 7278
Mulberry Hill B/B 033 330 5921
Nottingham Road Hotel 033 266 6151
Old Halliwell Country Inn 033 330 2606
Penny Lane Guesthouse 033 234 4332
Pleasant Places 033 234 4396
Rawdons Hotel 033 266 6044
Sierra Ranch B/B 033 263 1073
Siteka Lodge 033 330 2073
Stillwater Lodge 033 267 7280
Stonehaven Farm B/B 033 263 2632
Tamakwa Country Lodge 033 267 7154 B/B
Thatchings B/B 033 266 6275

Colourful products of the Shuttleworth Weavers.

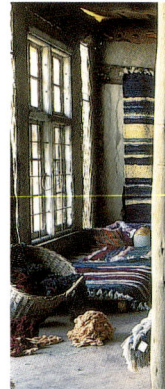

The ghost of room seven at the famed Nottingham Road Hotel (Notties) is not as welcoming as the patron and less cheerful than the bar staff!

Midlands Meander

73

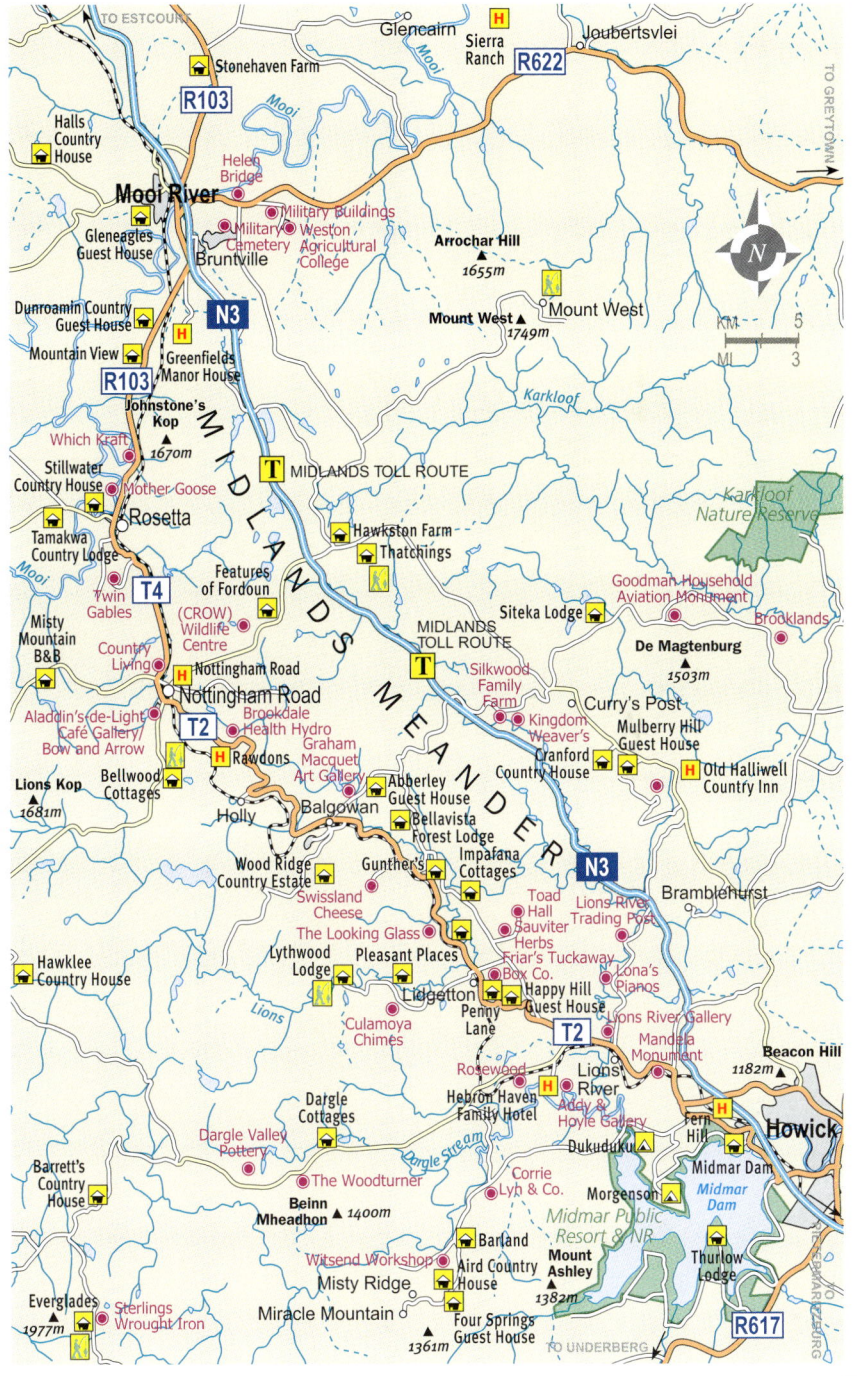

The self-proclaimed 'gateway to the Midlands', Mooi River (which means beautiful river) is a perfect base camp and stopover point for travellers.

Mooi River

Mooi River's ornate railway station was once the hub of railway traffic throughout the Midlands, but things have quietened down as other forms of transport have taken over. The Station Master's Arms is a great place to keep your eye on the track as you enjoy a bite to eat and perhaps a sip of something sweet. Rhode House Museum includes exhibits that honour the local dairy industry, while the Weston Agricultural College Museum has photographs and a cache of memorabilia documenting local history. St Johns Church (on the Weston Road) harks back to 1872 and has stood firm through two wars – testament to the quality of the locally-made bricks. Mooirivier Falls suffers an 80m drop over a rocky gorge on the Mooirivier ... but don't think you can just drop in on the falls: it's view by appointment only!

The Mooi river, close to Rosetta.

BLAZING SADDLES
With great fishing and other Midlands-like activities all around, this little colonial outpost understandably boasts one of Africa's greatest polo clubs. Karkloof Polo Club bears a proud history, and the members enjoy magnificent scenery from their three polo fields. Staying in the saddle, the district around Mooi River is rich in high-class stud farms that feed the hungry Natal horseracing circuit. Summerhill Farm is one of the more prestigious, and visits to studs can usually be arranged.

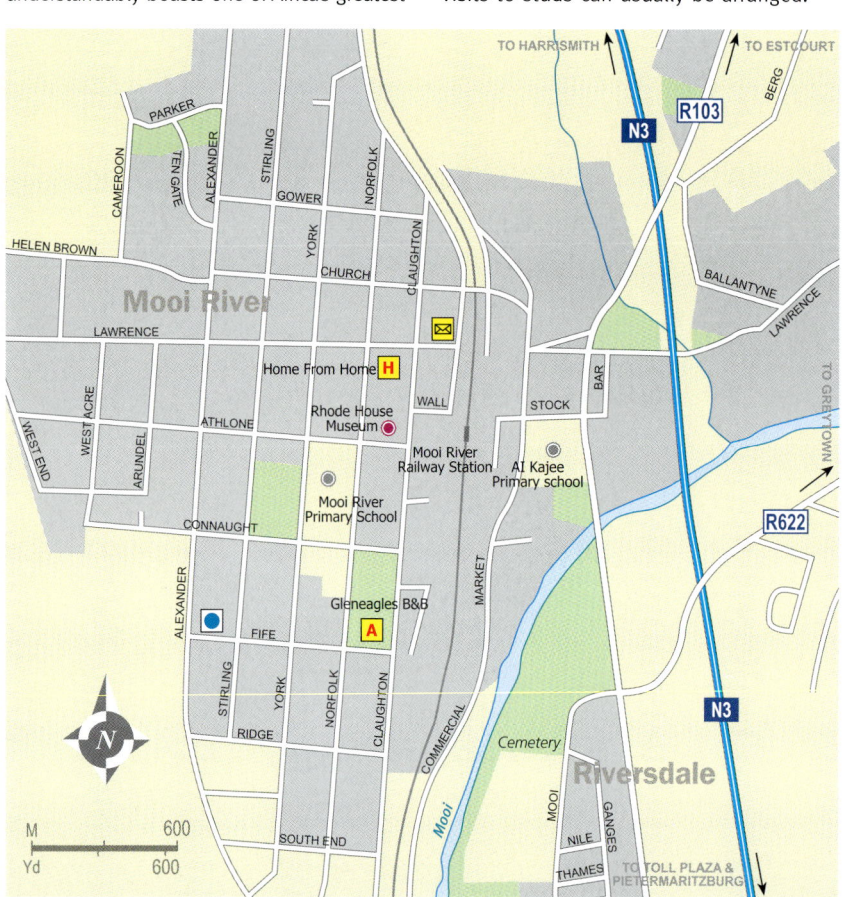

Humans have slept at the stunning Sewula (with its dramatic natural features) for at least a thousand years.

Bushmans River Region Bushmans

The history of the area around Sewula dates back to fossils and the arrival of early humans like the Bushmen. Much historial research has been carried out (not to mention scraping and digging by paleontologists and archaeologists), particularly in the catchment area of the Bushmans River. From the comfort of a vehicle you can drive to the Drakensberg, enjoy the Midlands Meander and view historic battlefields. Indigenous trees abound and there are delightful pools and cliffs in the Bushman's River bed, where fish, crabs and clawless otter enjoy the cool waters. The river is also a popular venue for river (and white-water) rafting, with great scenery and some even greater challenges facing you on the water. If that's not your kettle of fish, then how about taking a turn on one of the 4x4 or MTB trails, or abseiling ... or even braving a ride on a foofy slide? You can't say there's no choice out here in this neck of the wilds!

The region offers the perfect setting for horseback safaris.

Top Tip

Sewula Gorge Lodge offers modern, serviced self-catering at its best, in a dramatic gorge with a waterfall and glorious countryside, as well as access to a Bald Ibis nesting colony.

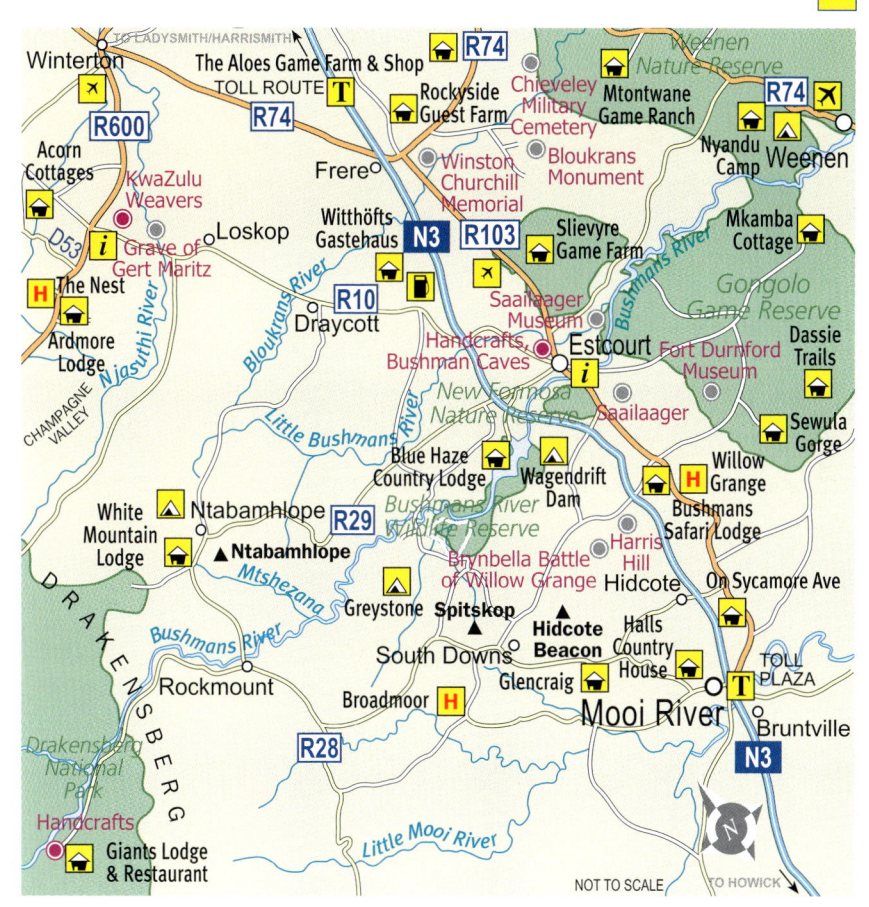

75

South Africa's second-oldest European settlement, Weenen stands for 'weeping' – it was the site of a horrendous Zulu massacre of Voortrekkers.

Estcourt Weenen Nature Reserve

ESTCOURT

Estcourt was founded as a stopover town on the long route from Durban into the interior and has seen its share of conflict over the decades, but now enjoys life as an agricultural and industrial hub. There are many hiking opportunities outside of town and a smattering of smaller nature reserves, but the town itself is worth exploring. Glamosa Glass offers glass-making tours, and local operators run tours of Zulu cultural villages. Historic buildings include the Old Civic Buildings and the ornate Old Magistrate's Residency, while the Powder Magazine dates back to 1859. Fort Durnford (with its engrossing museum) was erected in 1874, and the Railway Bridge first carried passengers in 1885. The Augustinian Chapel was built in 1929, while the beautiful St Matthews Anglican Church was the town's second church. The Brynbella-Willow Grange battlesite near town saw unfriendly fire between Boer and Brit in the Anglo-Boer War.

WEENEN

The Weenen Museum has some priceless Voortrekker antiquities yet even more special is the building itself, built by Andries Pretorius, the famed Voortrekker leader.

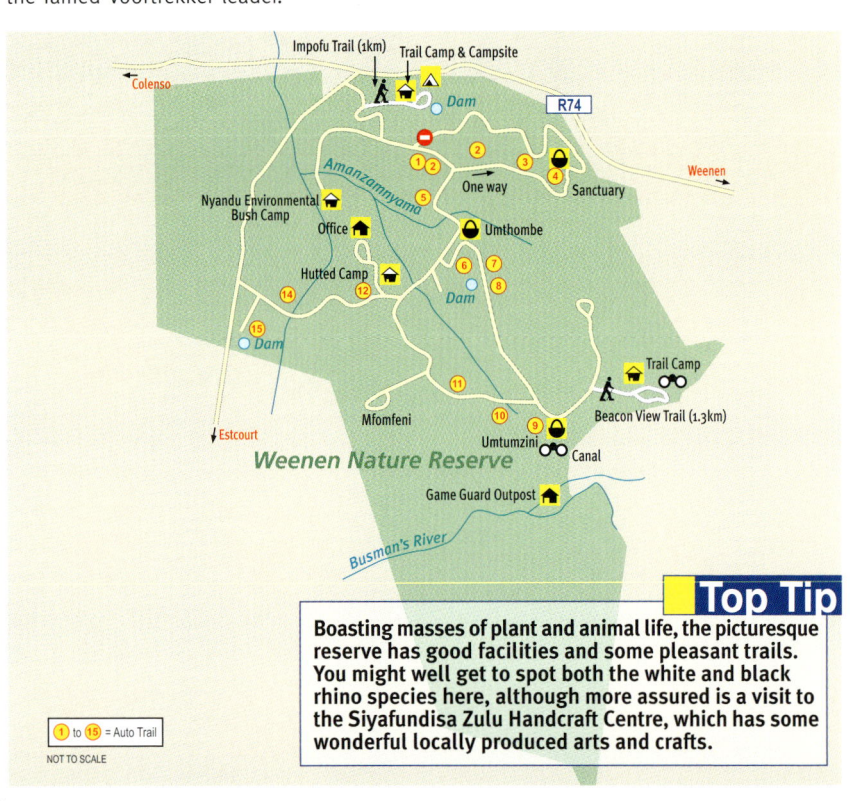

Top Tip

Boasting masses of plant and animal life, the picturesque reserve has good facilities and some pleasant trails. You might well get to spot both the white and black rhino species here, although more assured is a visit to the Siyafundisa Zulu Handcraft Centre, which has some wonderful locally produced arts and crafts.

Spioenkop has a wealth of wildlife that you can view from your car, including zebra, rhino, giraffe and a variety of buck.

Winterton Bergville Spioenkop Dam

Nestling in the Drakensberg foothills, Bergville ('mountain village') is a typical small pioneer town, relaxed yet welcoming. Many of its buildings have been restored to pay homage to the brave early pioneers. Bergville is ideally positioned for exploring the northern parts of the park and the battlefields areas. A short drive away is Spioenkop (battlefield, nature reserve and dam), the Rangeworthy Cemetery (resting place for victims at Spioenkop and Bastion Hill) and the Woodstock Dam. En route to the Royal Natal National Park is Thandanani Craft Village with its traditional baskets, beadwork and woodwork. Winterton is a pretty village set in beautiful countryside and is an ideal launch pad for visits to the northern and central 'Berg. The Winterton Museum has a superb Anglo-Boer War library, local history exhibits, a replica tribal homestead exhibit, as well as geology, fauna and flora displays.

Spioenkop Dam.

Top Tip
Make an effort to be in town on the third Friday of every month and enjoy the spectacle and atmosphere of Bergville's cattle sales. Just be careful not to keep waving those flies away!

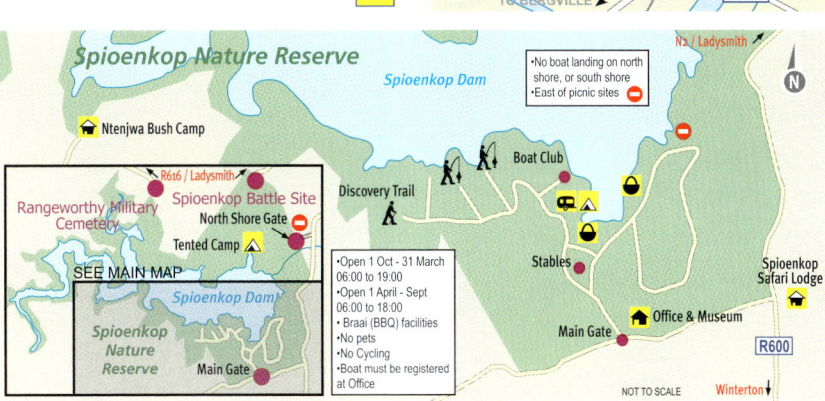

77

Sign the mountain register before you leave your hotel and never hike or climb in a group of fewer than three individuals.

Drakensberg

THE DRAKENSBERG REGION

The Drakensberg, a landscape of giant peaks, dramatic rock formations, tumbling falls, indigenous forests, rolling streams and misty mornings, is one of South Africa's great adventure playgrounds for young and old, active and social, local or foreigner. Formally known as uKhahlamba Drakensberg Park, the enormous biological diversity and scores of endangered species, in addition to the natural beauty of the varied landscape and the cultural heritage of prolific San rock art images, has deservedly earned the park World Heritage Site status. This diverse and dramatic escarpment straddles the KwaZulu-Natal border of South Africa and that of the 'mountain kingdom' of Lesotho (as well as pushing into the Eastern Cape and the Free State) and covers more than 5,000km² of land within easy reach of dozens of villages, towns and cities. The Drakensberg is accessible geographically and physically, making it a highly popular destination: you can reach it without abandoning civilisation for days on end, and can choose between a guided tour of a few hours, some rough and tumble adrenaline pursuits, gentle hikes, bike or horse rides, carefree trout fishing, or more rugged camping and mountaineering. The choices are many, and the results hugely rewarding and monumentally memorable, not least for the magnificent scenery and tranquility that may well be equalled by some of the world's other great wilderness areas, but it surely can't be beaten.

Clematis Brachiata, aka Traveller's joy – its leaves are packed into weary shoes to ease blisters, aches and pains.

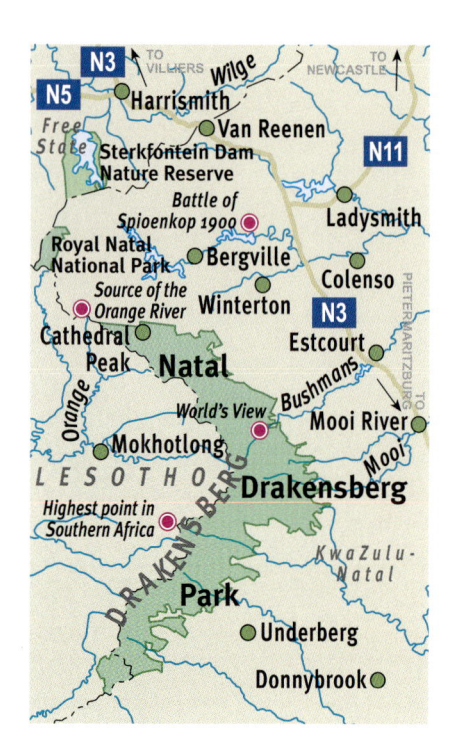

Loteni Nature Reserve.

The Maletsunyane Falls near Semonkong is southern Africa's highest 'single-drop' falls, tipping down from higher than 190m.

Lesotho

Roughly 80 percent of this small kingdom's land (30,000km²) is made up of rugged mountains, which explains the proliferation of friendly, blanket-clad Basotho people leading their ponies around (often with a tourist in the saddle!). Known as 'the kingdom in the sky', landlocked Lesotho holds the record for the world's 'highest lowest' point – 1400m above sea level. Part of the Drakensberg range that crosses into Lesotho (linked by the Sani Pass) Thabana Ntlenyana means 'beautiful little mountain' ... yet this highest peak in southern Africa reaches up to a height of 3,482m above sea level. Beautiful scenery, winter snowfall, over 300 days of sunshine a year, and some rugged scenery to tackle (on foot, in the saddle or behind the wheel of a 4x4) make Lesotho a great diversion for tourists and locals. There's also a wealth of San rock art and even dinosaur tracks to astound the kids or keep the geologically inclined out of trouble, while the local craft industry (notably at Maseru) offers a feast for hunters of exciting ethnic designs and authentic products.

Basotho people with their traditional blankets.

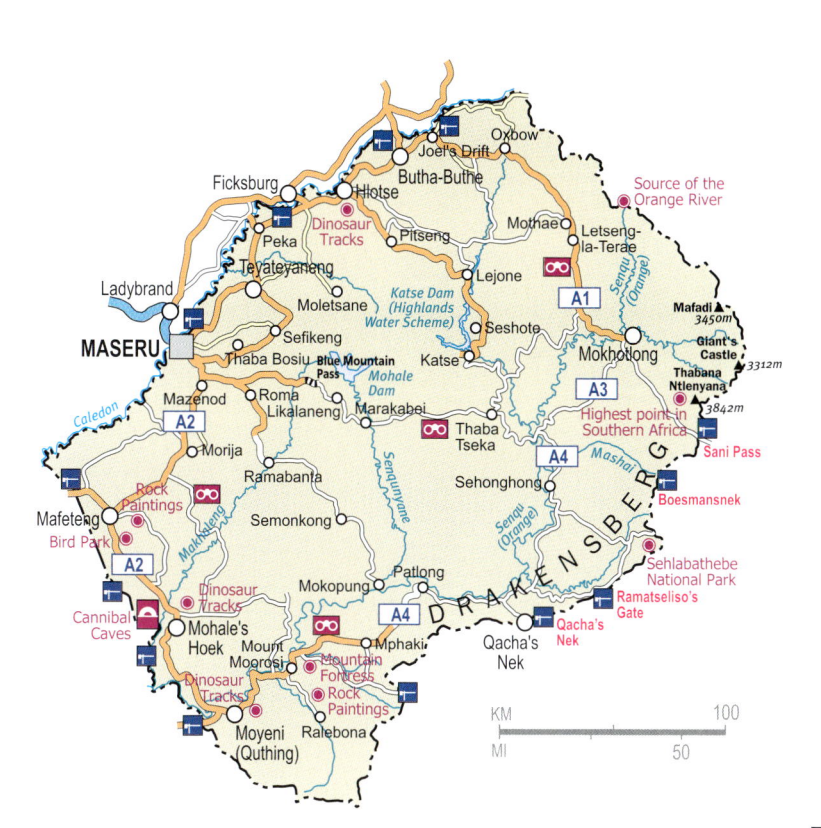

Always take warm clothing and a reasonable supply of food and water to keep you going in case of emergencies on the mountain.

Northern Drakensberg

A WHEEL GOOD TIME
There are numerous biking trails to enjoy in the Drakensberg, notably the 35km Mike's Pass mountain bike trail in the Cathedral Peak region. Awe-inspiring beauty and views are presented on this trail ... if you have time to look as you navigate a number of the steep climbs and face the hair-raising 7km downhill charge.

THE WONDERS OF WATERFALLS
If you enjoy the spectacle of a natural waterfall then you will be in your element in the Drakensberg. The area is blessed with waterfalls of every shape, size and power, most famously the legendary Tugela Falls, all 850m of it (one of the highest falls in the world): its name, appropriately, means 'the startling one'! A waterfall presents a haven for footsore hikers, walkers or bikers who'll enjoy the excuse of 'sampling nature' to rest up within the tranquility of the tumbling water and its natural swimming facilities. Waterfalls also boast an entire microclimate and environment that attracts an abundance of plant, animal and bird life. It's a bit like satellite TV for nature lovers!

LOOKING FOR LARGE?
Cathkin Farm (near Bell Park Dam) has the largest Paperbark Thorn tree in the entire southern hemisphere. Its canopy stretches across almost 35m, and its woody pods provide food for cattle and game. Its thorns are rumoured to be poisonous ... so don't eat them!

Top Tip
Take a drive out to visit the nearby Drakensberg Boys Choir School. These world-famous vocal angels offer visitors twice-weekly concerts.

Top: *Hiking in the Royal National Park.*
Above: *Amphitheatre covered in snow.*
Below: *Cathedral Peak (Mlambonja wilderness area).*

> The mountain's great size and its height above sea level contribute to extremely unpredictable weather. Not even locals gamble on the weather!

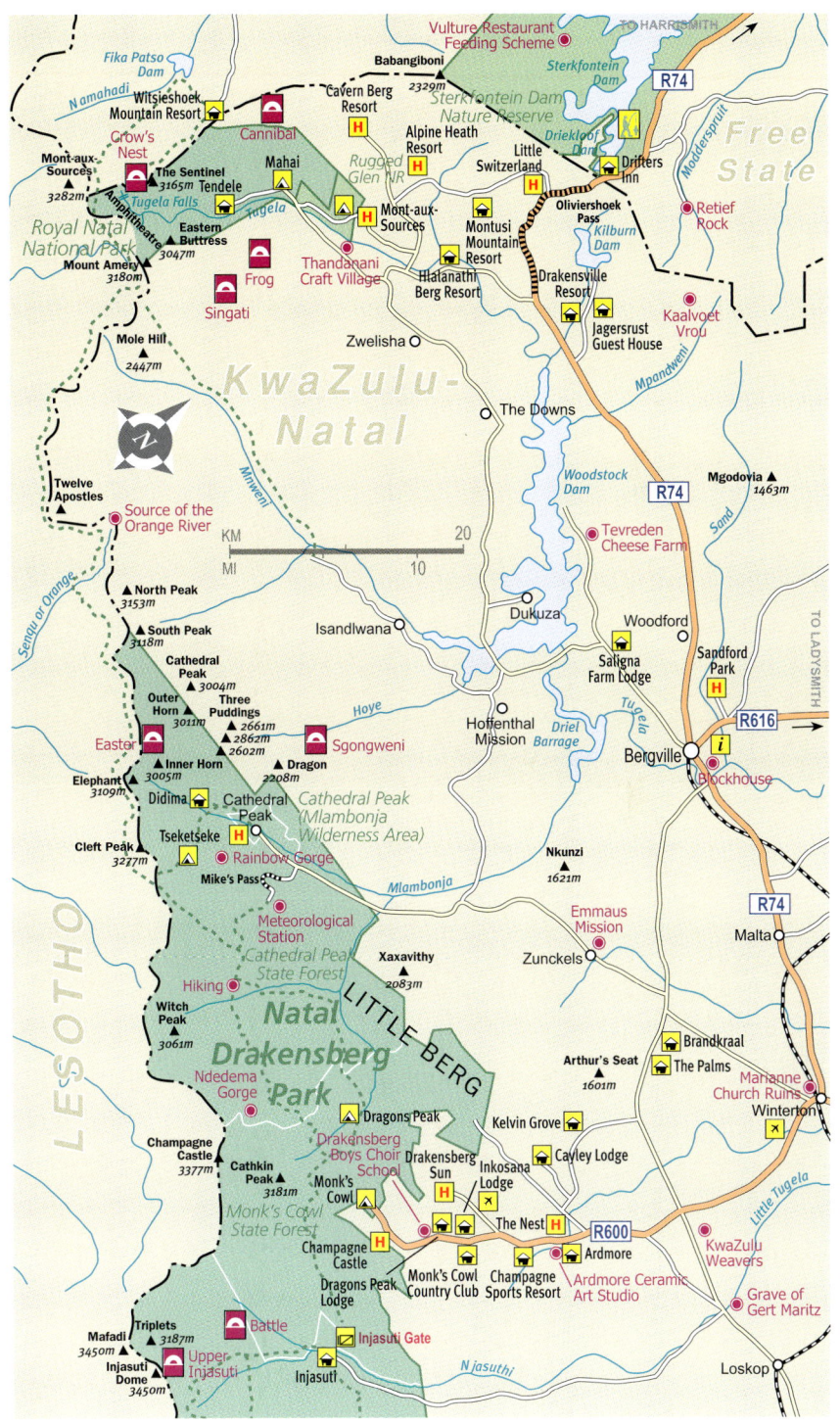

Northern Drakensberg

No live bait may be used to catch trout in the Drakensberg — it's flies or nothing for the 6,000-plus who cast their lines annually!

Central Drakensberg

ROCKY ONE
Bushman paintings are a major drawcard for tourists, and there's plenty to behold, with around 600 rock sites featuring around 40,000 paintings. Protected by law, these artworks are extremely fragile — touching is out of the question, but smoke from fires and other human interventions can also cause damage (which will attract a large fine or jail time). Calls of nature should be expressed at least five minutes away from a cave, preferably in grassland.

DROP BY FOR LUNCH SOMETIME
During the 1820s smaller tribes were forced to flee from Shaka Zulu's impis who ran rampant across KwaZulu-Natal. Many found refuge in caves throughout the mountain range and eventually resorted to cannibalism in order to survive — hence the aptly named Cannibal Cave.

Top: *Injasuti, Zulu homes.*
Centre: *Vulture at Giant's Castle.*
Left: *Rest camp in Giant's Castle area.*

The original Zulu name for the mountain range was uKhahlamba, but the mountain (berg) reminded the Boers of a dragon (draken).

Central Drakensberg

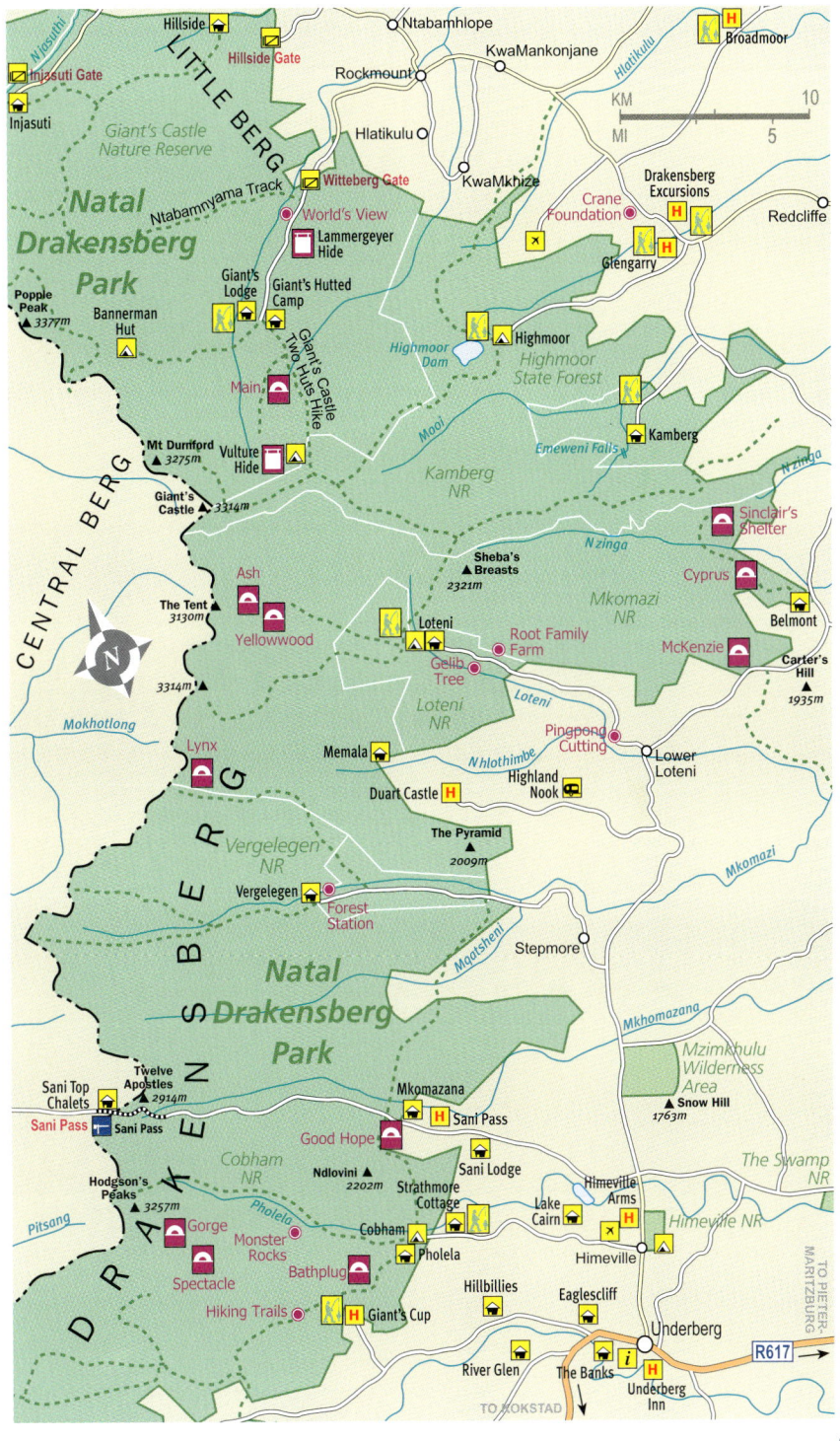

Horse riding outings in the Drakensberg vary from canters of a couple of hours to treks (journeys) of a few days.

Southern Drakensberg

FAUNA AND FLORA
Visitors might think that the Drakensberg must have won Nature's Lottery, considering its amazing biological diversity: well over 2,100 plant species, around 300 varieties of bird life, almost 50 species of mammal and reptile apiece, as well as nearly 30 types of frog. Sadly, well over 100 of all these natural treasures feature in the Red Book ... the list of endangered species. All visitors should respect the nature around them.

HIGHS & LOWS
The Drakensberg range has a number of famous peaks dotted across the escarpment: Cathedral Peak (3,004m), Devil's Knuckles (3,028m), Eastern Buttress (3,047m), Cathkin Peak (3,181m), Hodgson's Peaks (3,257m), Mont-aux-Sources (3,282m), Giant's Castle (3,314m), Champagne Castle (3,377m) and Thabana Ntlenyana (3,482m — Southern Africa's highest point).

MONT-AUX-SOURCES
Meaning 'the mountain of springs', Zulus and Basothos call it emPhofeni and Pofung respectively ('place of the eland'). Named by two French missionaries in 1836, Mont-aux-Sources is the source of five major rivers (including the Tugela and Orange) — and as it stands 3,282m above sea level it naturally sparks off numerous spectacular waterfalls down the sheer mountain walls.

Eland Valley resort.

Top Tip
The best time to visit the Drakensberg is in winter. Why? The atmosphere is at its best as the air is fresh and crisp, guaranteed to pump life into all your senses. Pack warm clothes!

Lake Naverone with Rhino Peak in the background.

Plowman's Kop (2,010m) offers spectacular views for brave hikers who have the guts to clamber up through 'The Crack'.

Southern Drakensberg

85

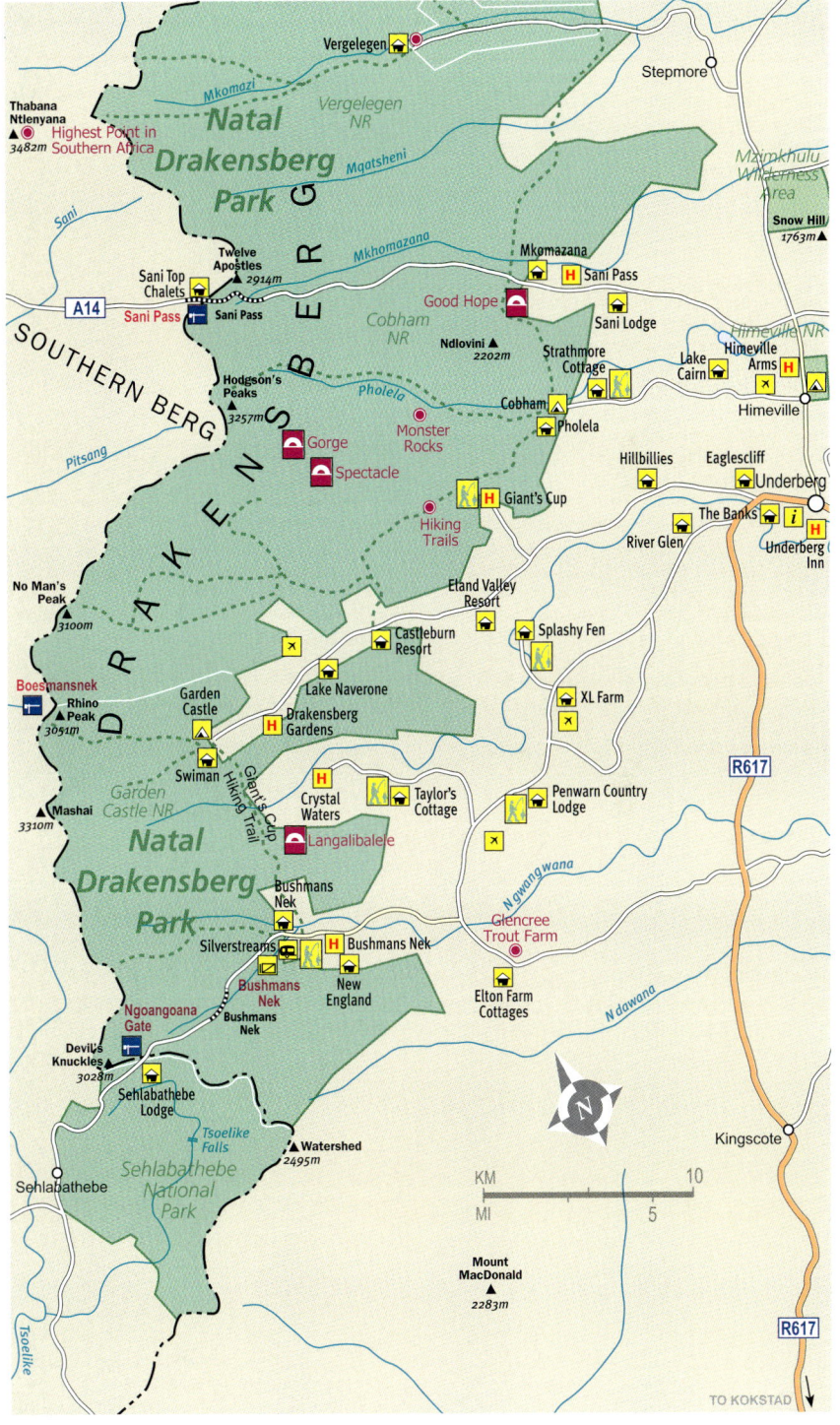

For 80 years war raged through the KwaZulu-Natal countryside, bloody conflicts being waged between Boers, Brits and the Zulus.

Battlefields Battlefields Battlefields

The Battlefields Region

The peace that currently drifts across this rolling and lush countryside belies the grim and brutal fighting that took place throughout most of the 1800s. The Battlefields Route takes visitors through hundreds of kilometres of road, allowing time to enjoy and indulge in the small, unusual and dramatic towns that dot the landscape, each with their own history, mystery and dramas to recount ... as well as bed and breakfast at the ready! With so much desolate surrounding countryside it really allows you to let your mind wander and imagine what it must have been like to face an army of attacking Zulu warriors, sunburnt British soldiers, or crafty Boer horsemen. The quiet surrounds allow you to reflect on the tragic loss of life spawned by armed conflict and greed for land.

RORKE'S DRIFT
The Rorke's Drift Museum pays homage to a mighty British defence: 100 soldiers kept 4000 Zulu warriors at bay for 12 hours, earning them 11 Victoria crosses (presumably not to share!).

BLOOD RIVER
The life-size statues of a semi-circle of a wagon laager provides an awesome monument of this great battle that saw so much loss of life that the victorious Boers proclaimed that the Ncome River ran red with Zulu blood.

ISANDLWANA
In response to an invasion of their land (which was an attempt to conquer the mighty Zulu nation), 25,000 Zulu impis defeated the 24th Regiment on 22 January 1879. Their

Aloes watching over the Tugela River.

attack was delayed as they waited for the right phase of the moon, and they employed their trademark pincer movement to overthrow the British.

LADYSMITH
Besieged by Boer general Piet Joubert for almost four months, keeping 12,000 British troops effectively 'prisoners'. Not to be passed up is a visit to the excellent Seige Museum on Murchison Street (and take a look at the four field guns outside).

Top Tip
The engrossing Talana Museum was built to commemorate the 1899 Battle of Talana. Audio tape 'tour guides' are available at Talana and at Fugitives Drift.

Graves, Elandslaagte.

The Battlefields Route is extremely popular with local and overseas visitors, with over 50 sites of interest to choose from across the countryside.

Battlefields Battlefields Battlefields

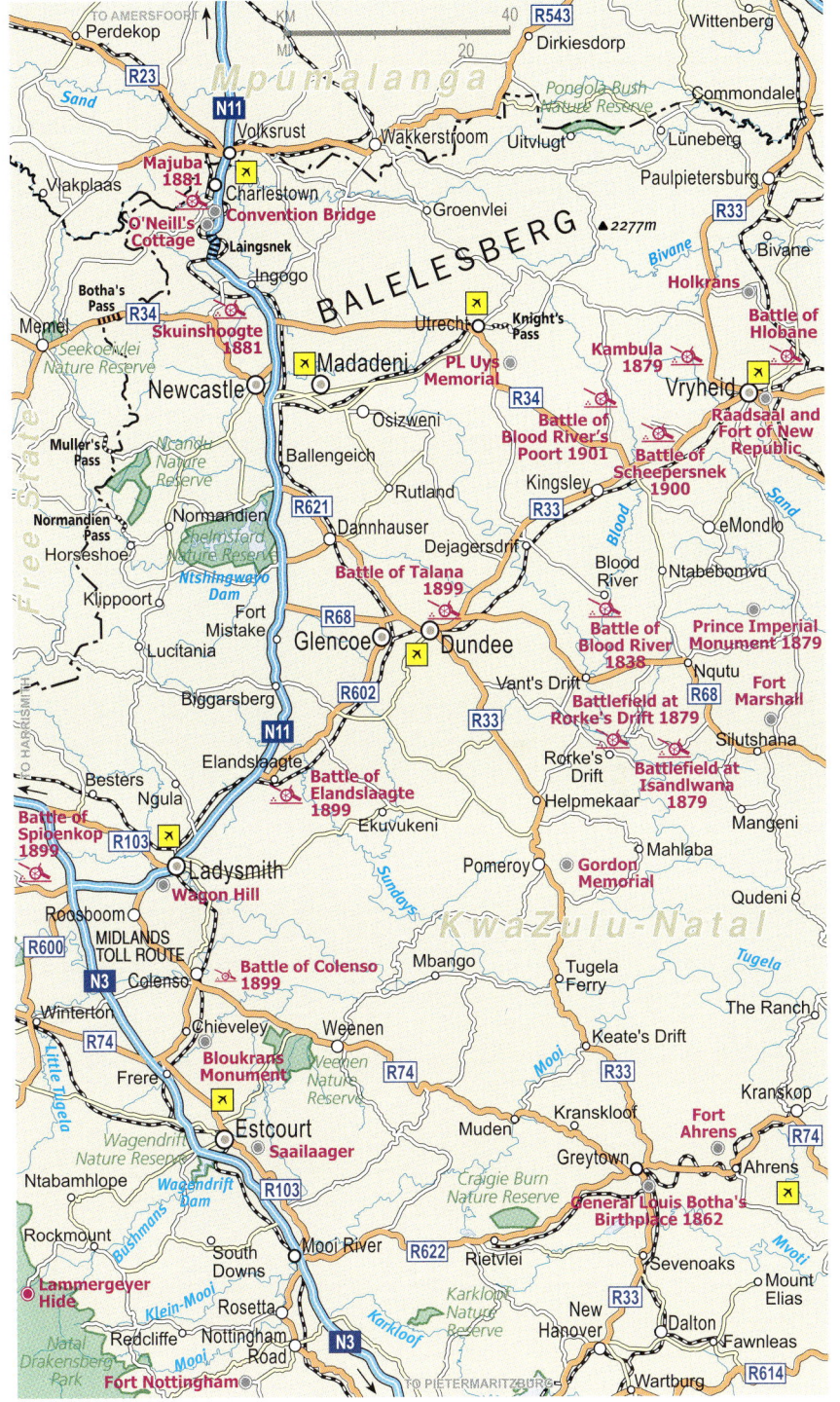

The RE Stevenson Museum (on the Bulwer Bridge) records the mighty battles in the Colenso area ... and the key is kept at the local police station!

Greytown Colenso Greytown Cole

GREYTOWN
Known as the 'Place of the Little Elephant', Greytown is the hub around which roads to Colenso, Mooi River, Stanger, Pietermaritzburg and Dundee spread out. The Greytown Museum (appropriately, on Voortrekker Street) features a diverse mix of cultural heritage and history, as well as a replica military room, an old blacksmith's forge and an array of ancient farmyard equipment, a Cape cart and spider, cannons and an old hearse. There's even a cannon brought to the town in 1852 by a teenage girl, aided by a small team of shipwrecked Zulus.

COLENSO
Flanked in parts by the R103 and the Tugela River, Colenso (and the Tugela) is famous for its role in the battlefields history. General Louis Botha's 6000 Boer commandos repelled 16,000 British troops: 1100 British soldiers died, yet just 8 Boer lives were lost!

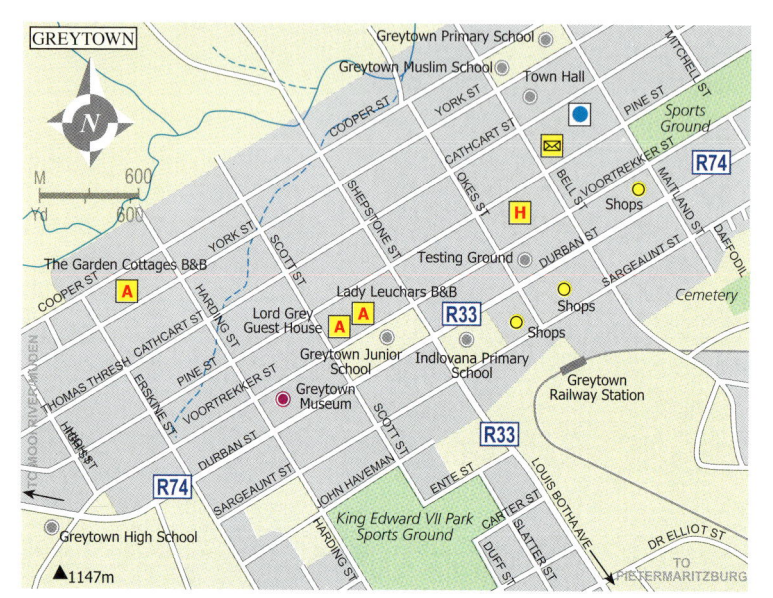

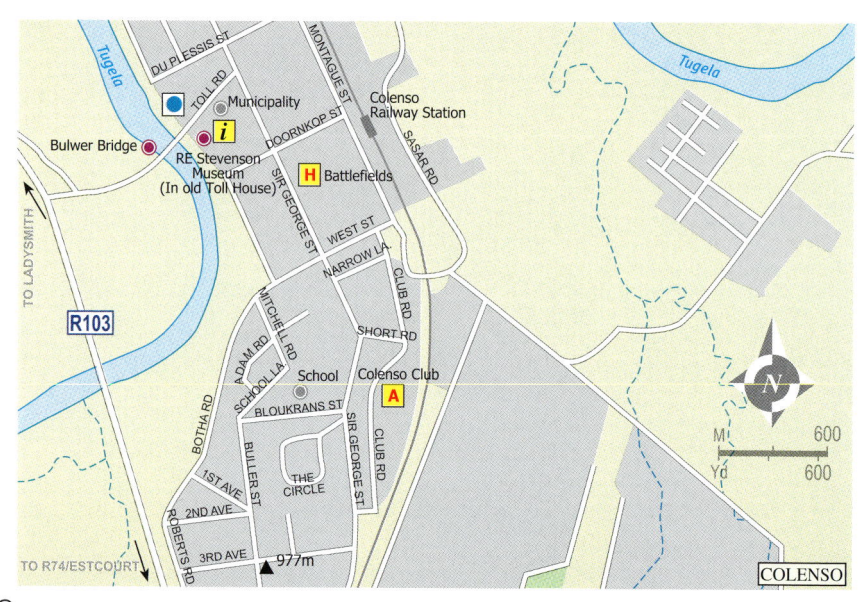

A Beer Route on the Hattingspruit Road serves up locally brewed German beer ... a calming diversion from the intensity of the Battlefields Route.

Ladysmith Dundee Ladysmith Dund

LADYSMITH
The Klip River runs through this small, rural town. The Seige Museum (see page 86) is a must-visit, and the town hall museum presents a local photographic history. Other sites include a Zulu fort, the Gandhi statue, Long Tom gun replicas and the stunning Soofi Mosque. The cultural museum on Keate Street pays tribute to the Drakensberg Boys Choir and Ladysmith Black Mambaza, one of SA's most successful music bands.

DUNDEE
Close to many battlesites and boasting the comprehensive Talana Museum (see page 86), Dundee has plenty of historic buildings to visit and photograph, such as the Cenotaph memorial for World War victims, a MOTH Museum with superb war artifacts, and plenty of historic churches. There are also a host of country activities and adventures offered in the town's surrounds, including horse riding, 4x4 and hiking trails.

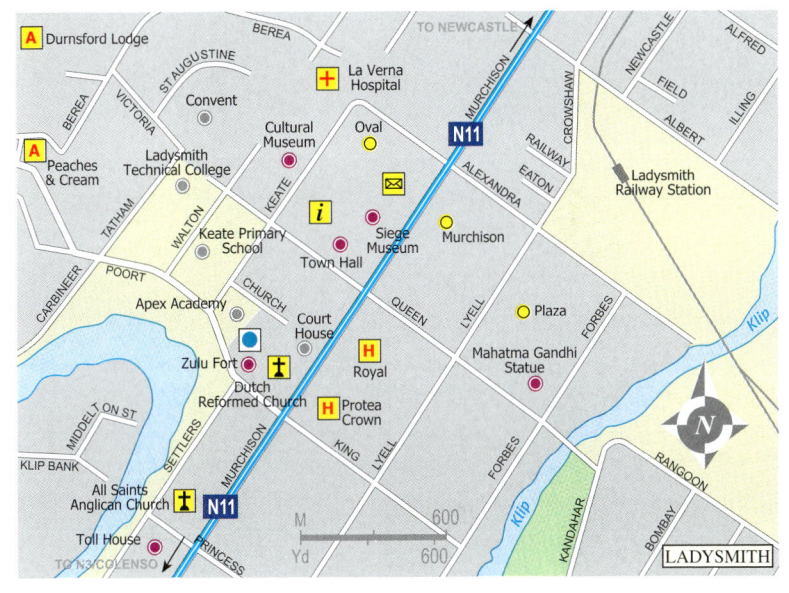

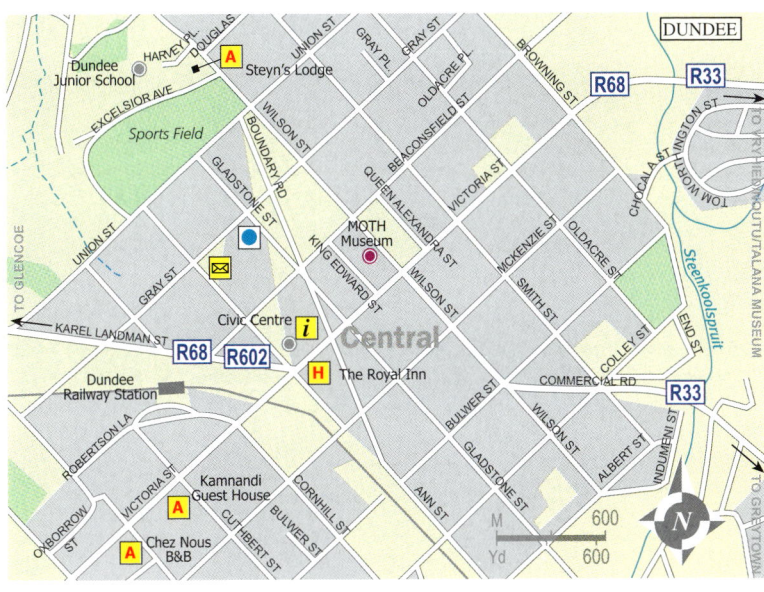

The town was founded when a honeymooning doctor from Newcastle in England was held prisoner by the overflowing Ncandu River.

Newcastle

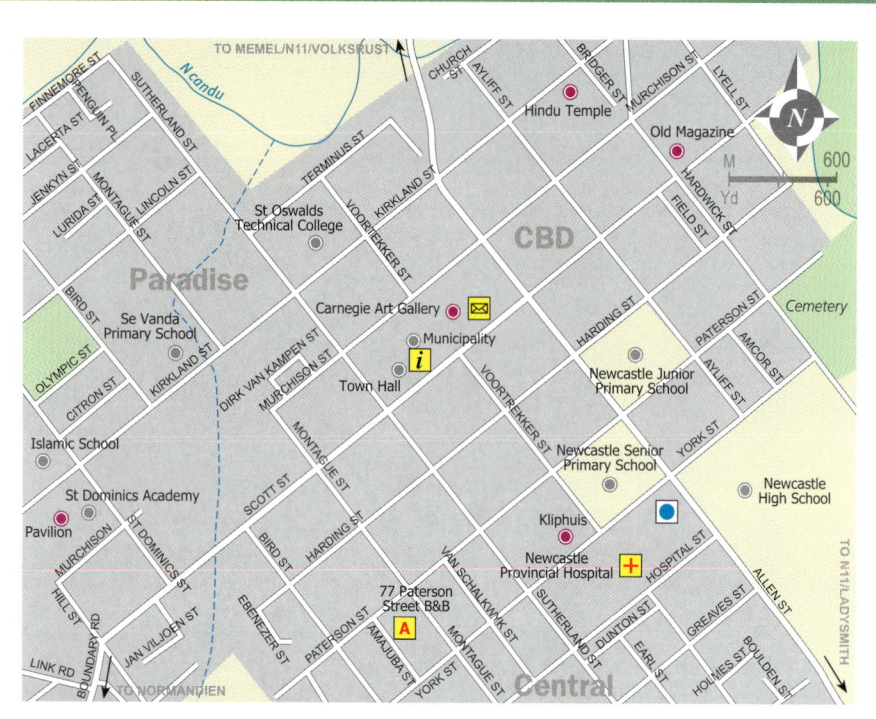

Chelmsford boasts the largest population of the rare Oribi in South Africa.

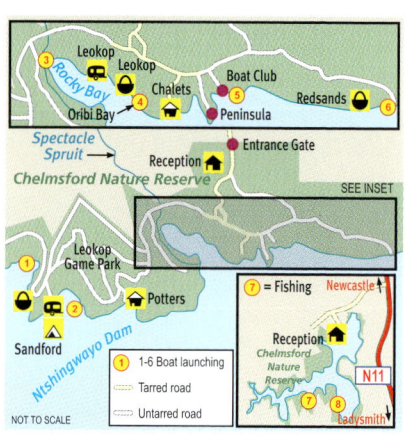

The mountains surrounding Newcastle are great hiking venues, and the peaks of Koningsberg and Kanskop both reach up more than 2000m. Hilldrop House is a National Monument as is the former home of author Rider Haggard. Haggard's life and work is documented in the museum at Fort Amiel (1876), which was built to stave off Zulu advances. Fort Terror is one of a number of signalling posts in the area, while another National Monument is St Dominics Pavilion (1916), originally built as a skating rink and social hub.

CHELMSFORD NATURE RESERVE

Surrounding the 3400ha Ntshingwayo Dam (a watersport and fishing haven, with chalets on the waters edge), Chelmsford is home to SA's largest population of rare oribi, and also presents visitors with great bird- and animal-watching experiences. There are no dangerous animals in Chelmsford: it's safe to walk or cycle around the reserve.

The picturesque Balele Mountains hide the town of Utrecht, a veritable gem for tourists, and located within a game park.

Utrecht

UTRECHT

Named after a town in the Netherlands, Utrecht is a charming and historic town which still shows signs of the original irrigation systems that are over 100 years old. KZN's premier wool-producing area, the town offers visitors plenty of historic buildings, monuments and historic sites to visit. A walk around town for a few hours on one of the many organized walks will take you back in time to the late 1800s, especially with some of the colonial masterpieces to view, notably Rothman, Shawe and Uys houses. Architectural treats abound in Utrecht. The town's cemetery looks after Boer and Brit soliders buried amongst one another, the Old Gaol is worth a visit, while the Old Parsonage Museum (1888) stores a rich cache of Boer War treasures. The interior of the Anglican church is spectacular, while the Mangosuthu arts and crafts centre offers fabulous crafts made by local hands (wood-carved dishes, woven grass mats, terracotta pots and ceramics).

A zebra's stripes are totally unique, like human fingerprints.

BALELE GAME PARK

Spread over 2500ha (including the surrounding mountains), the park has been stocked with over a dozen species of game (buck, zebra and giraffe). The long-term goal is to encourage the game to wander around on the outskirts of town. Game drives, birding tours and a range of sporting activities can all be indulged in here.

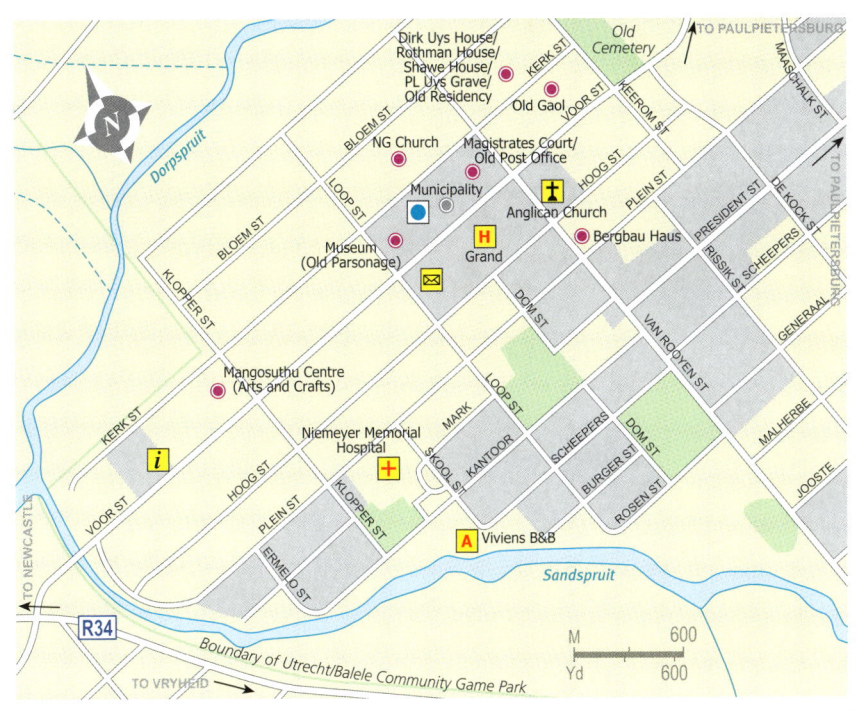

Vryheid means "freedom" or "liberty", and the eye-stretching horizons in the area back up this moniker.

Vryheid

Historic buildings are somewhat in abundance in Vryheid, including the Dutch Reformed Church (and its typical architecture), Fort Vryheid (a National Monument), Evangelical Lutheran churches (built by the German community) and the Old Raadsaal (1884) with an old fort and jail riding on its coattails, and the Anglo-Boer War Memorial. The Nuwe Republiek (New Republic) Museum is housed in the Old Raadsaal. The flamboyant Carnegie Public Library (1909) was restored for the town's centenary celebrations and now houses Vryheid's info bureau, while the Cecil Emmett Park provides the family with a good day's activities.

PUTTING THEIR STAMP ON IT
In the early days of the Republic Vryheid produced a range of hand-made stamps, a full set of which can be viewed at the Lucas Meyer museum. The museum is found in the Cape Dutch Revivalist-styled house built for the widow of the Republic's first president.

The Jack and Jill Hiking Club will be a good ally to you in planning and executing your hikes in the countryside around Vryheid.

Vryheid Hill Nature Reserve

VRYHEID HILL NATURE RESERVE

Offers a one-day hiking trail with fantastic scenery and the chance to catch a breather at the old Anglo-Boer War gun points. The reserve has numerous game (blesbuck, impala, eland, Burchell's zebra, mountain reedbuck, oribi and duiker, as well as more than 30 other species of mammal), over 200 bird species, 80-plus types of tree, 30 grass species and 20 types of reptile. The 4km hiking trail will open up fabulous scenery. The Ntingonono Environmental Centre offers tours guaranteed to expand your knowledge.

OVER THE HILL?

Lancaster Hill (aka Vryheid Hill) has been home to man for thousands of years, and their daily tools can still be seen. It also saw action on 11 December 1900, when the Lancaster Regiment kept the Boers at bay.

White-breasted cormorant are common residents along with several other bird species.

Top Tip
The incredibly 'rich' Vryheid Birding Route includes Vryheid Hill NR, Pongola Bush NR, Natal Spa, Skurweberg, Klipfontein Bird Sanctuary and Mpofini Game Lodge.

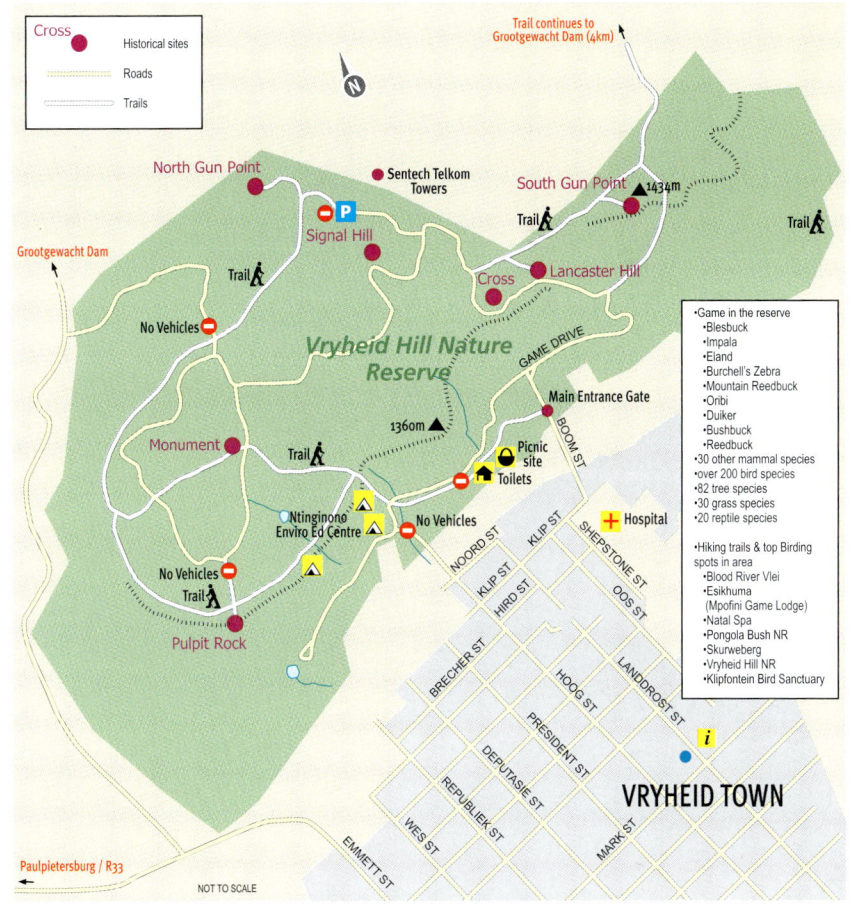

Map Legend
- Cross — Historical sites
- Roads
- Trails

Key locations: North Gun Point, Sentech Telkom Towers, South Gun Point (1434m), Signal Hill, Lancaster Hill (Cross), Grootgewacht Dam, Monument, Vryheid Hill Nature Reserve (1360m), Main Entrance Gate, Picnic site, Toilets, Ntinginono Enviro Ed Centre, Pulpit Rock, Hospital, Game Drive, Boom St.

Trail continues to Grootgewacht Dam (4km)

Game in the reserve
- Blesbuck
- Impala
- Eland
- Burchell's Zebra
- Mountain Reedbuck
- Oribi
- Duiker
- Bushbuck
- Reedbuck
- 30 other mammal species
- over 200 bird species
- 82 tree species
- 30 grass species
- 20 reptile species

Hiking trails & top Birding spots in area
- Blood River Vlei
- Esikhuma (Mpofini Game Lodge)
- Natal Spa
- Pongola Bush NR
- Skurweberg
- Vryheid Hill NR
- Klipfontein Bird Sanctuary

VRYHEID TOWN

Streets: Brecher St, Klip St, Hird St, Noord St, Shepstone St, Oos St, Hoog St, Landdrost St, President St, Deputasie St, Republiek St, Wes St, Emmett St, Mark St.

Paulpietersburg / R33

NOT TO SCALE

The slithery Pongola River satisfies watersport and fishing nuts, and empties into the massive man-made lake in the reserve.

Paulpietersburg

The Dumbe Dam is a lovely watersports resort used prolifically by day-trippers. The Victorian-style Old Drostdy (now used by the local tourism department) is one of the town's earliest structures and is, obviously, a National Monument. The Reformed Church holds within it an interesting library … and locals believe that Paul Kruger donated some spare cash to assist with construction costs (I don't suppose he left any locked chests behind for safe-keeping …?).

The historic Peace Boulders commemorate General Louis Botha's 'selection meeting' to find his right-hand men to sign the Anglo-Boer War peace treaty alongside him. Less than 20km out of town is the Natal Spa, which employs the hot mineral springs from the Bivane River to do its healing work (the water apparently contains radio-active properties!).

PONGOLA BUSH NATURE RESERVE

After much conservation work the Reserve is once more home to a thriving population of game, as well as the Big Four (no lions here), hippo and croc, and over 350 bird species. For a rush of blood, take part in the reserve's elephant tracking program or help track a rhino on foot (leave the cellphone and portable radio at the campsite!).

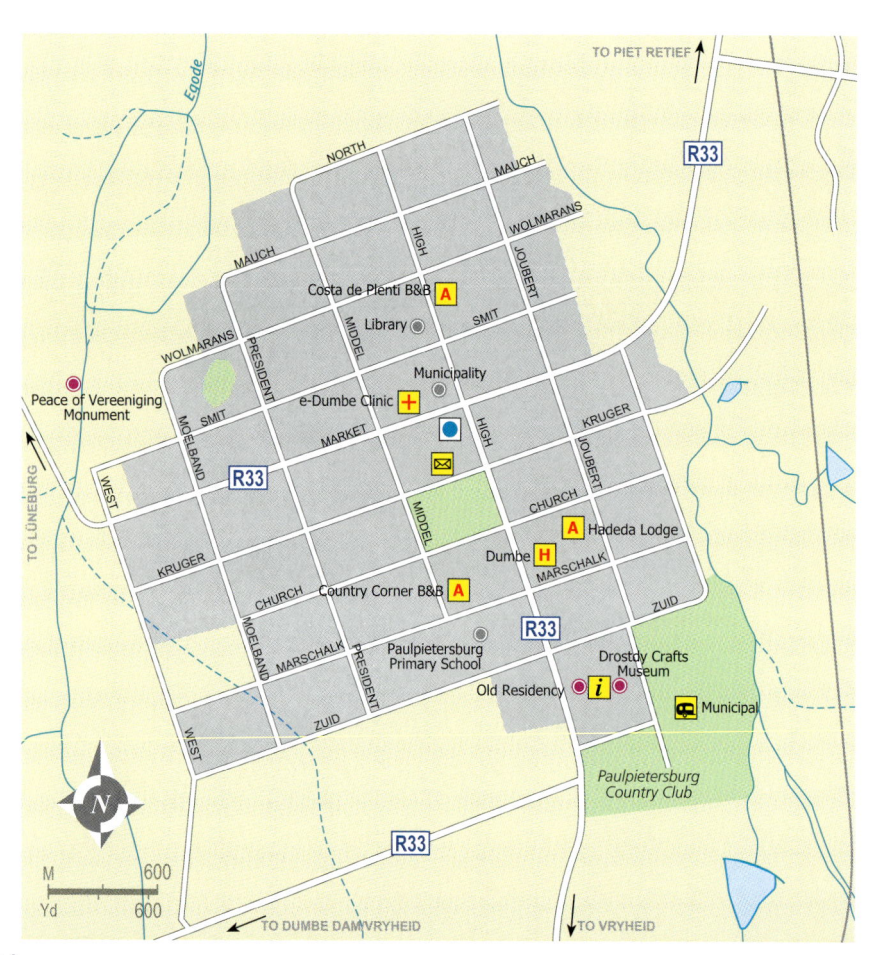

Ithala has gone from zero to hero in the 25 years since it was established and it is now one of KZN's premier nature reserves.

Ithala Game Reserve

Criss-crossed with rivers and many hiking options, this 30,000ha reserve is decorated with grassland, forested valleys and towering granite cliffs that stretch up to almost 1500m. The terrain has yielded a wide diversity of ecosystems, and this in turn has spawned a variety of wildlife, including giraffe, buck and zebra, the Big Four (again, no lion) – the latter are, however, somewhat tricky to track down. The varied plant life supports over 300 bird species, while winter bushveld trails and picnic spots add to the casual visitor's enjoyment and wildlife experience.

Top Tip: Ithala is a geological wonderland: its wide geological diversity includes some of the world's oldest rock formations (3000 million years old!).

Game drive in Ithala.

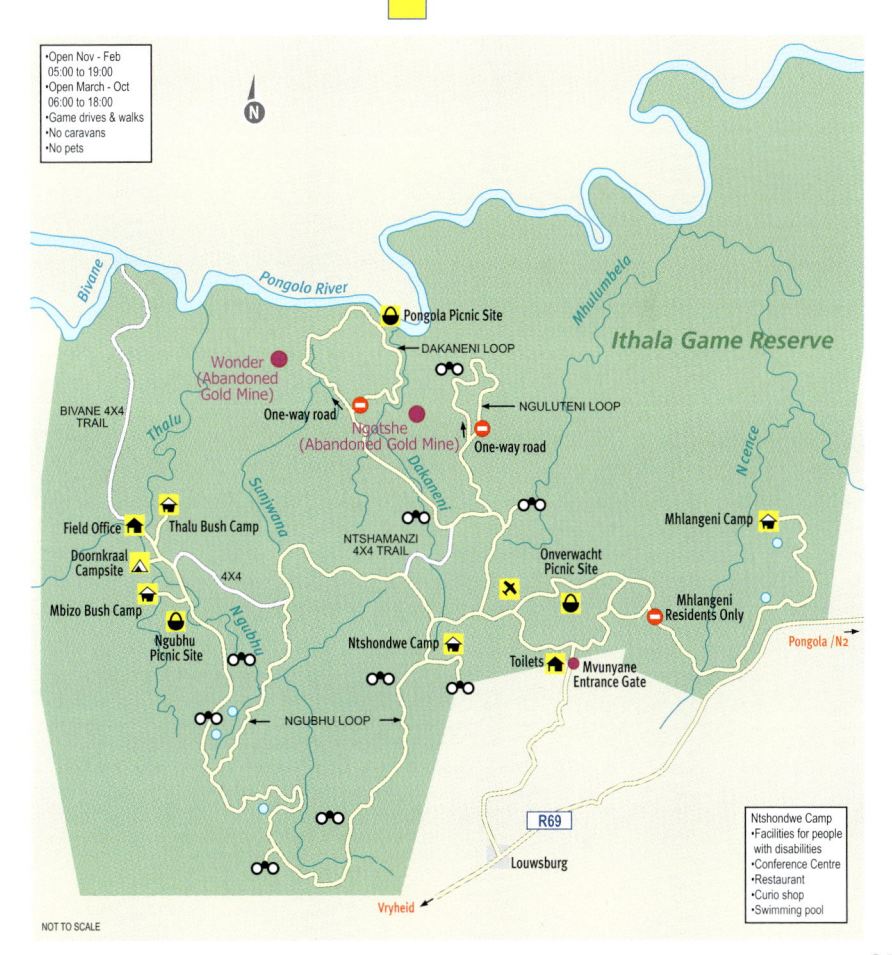

- Open Nov - Feb 05:00 to 19:00
- Open March - Oct 06:00 to 18:00
- Game drives & walks
- No caravans
- No pets

Ntshondwe Camp
- Facilities for people with disabilities
- Conference Centre
- Restaurant
- Curio shop
- Swimming pool

95

Touring Maps

C
D
100
98
LESOTHO
DRAKENSBERG
Linakeng
Mashai
Mqatsheni
Sani Pass
Sani Pass
Stepmore
Pholela
Himeville Nature Reserve
Himeville
A4
Sehonghong
Boesmansnek
Legooa
Natal Drakensberg Park
Underberg
Boesmans
Coleford Nature Reserve
Melikane
Sehlabathebe
Ngoangoana Gate
R617
Sehlabathebe National Park
Ndawana
Coleford
Tsoelike
Tsoelike
Gungununu
Kingscote
Ramatseliso's Gate
Qacha's Nek
Qacha's Nek
Mafube
Lehlohonolo
Swartberg
Driefontein
Beginsel
New Amalfi
Matatiele
Franklin
Cedarville
R56
Dorset
Mvenyane
Mount Currie Nature Reserve
R617
Adam Kok Memorial
Rustfontein
Kokstad
Mkemane
Colonanek
Brooks Nek
Eastern Cape
Fort Donald
Cabazi
Rode
Mount Ayliff
Mount Frere
Tina
Caba
Tabankulu
Mafusini
Mkumbi
N2
Culunca
Tina Bridge
Buwa
Sipetu
Flagstaff
R61

A
B
101
97
1
2
3
Lower Loteni
Impendle
Dargle
Midmar Dam
Queen Elizabeth Park
Hilton
Midmar Public Resort and Nature Reserve
Stepmore
Gomane
Edendale
Himeville Nature Reserve
Netherby
Boston
Elandskop
Himeville
R617
Pevensey
Underberg
Bulwer
Coleford Nature Reserve
Lovu
R56
Hella-Hella Pass
Mountain View
Ngudwini
Richmond
Donnybrook
Coleford
Soada Forest Nature Reserve
Eastwolds
Gungununu
Creighton
Bush Reserve
Lufafa
CJ Rhodes' House
R612
St Bernards
Ixopo
Nhlavini
Eastern Cape
R56
Highflats
Sneezewood
Umzimkulu
Mtwalume Falls
Mtwalume
Franklin
Little Bisi
Oetting
Bisi
Dorset
Bontrand
Bisi
Mzumbe
Goba
Stafford's Post
N2
St Faith's
Harding
KwaDweshula
Tungwa
N2
Mzimkulwana
Weza
Weza
Oribi Flats
Brooks Nek
Oribi Gorge Nature Reserve
Fort Donald
Mjika
Gangala
Mtamvuna
Nqabeni
Paddock
Bomela
Izingolweni
Ludeke
SOUTH COAST TOLL ROAD
Magusheni
Bizana
Umtamvuna
Ramsgate
Ngabeni
Southbroom
Redoubt
Mpenjati
R61
Eastern Cape
R61
Palm Beach
Mkumbi
Munster
Glenmore Beach
Mgodini
Mzamba
Umtamvuna Nature Reserve
Leisure Bay
Banners Rest
Port Edward
Mnyameni

Colenso Mission Station 1854
C
Nagle Dam
102
Ndwedwe
D
Ballito
Tongaat
Hazelmere Dam
Valley of 1000 Hills
PIETERMARITZBURG
Inanda
R102
N2
Verulam
Tongaat
Umdloti
Ashburton
Camperdown
Phoenix
KwaMashu
Umhlanga
R623
Thornville
N3
Krantzkloof Nature Reserve
Clermont
Hammarsdale
Mpumalanga
Marianhill
Pinetown
DURBAN
The Bluff
R603
Queensburgh
R624
Umlazi
Durban International Airport
Rosebank
Mid-Illovo
Umbumbulu
Adam's Mission
Amanzimtoti
Mkomazi
Lovu
Kingsburgh
N2
Umgababa
Dududu
Umkomaas
Clansthal
N cazuka
Vernon Crookes Nature Reserve
R102
R612
Umzinto
Scottburgh
Braemar
Park Rynie
Kelso
Pennington
Fafa
Friedenau
Ifafa
Sezela
Quha
Bazley
Mgeni
Ifafa Beach
St Joseph's
Glen Echo
R102
Mtwalume
Turton
Hibberdene
Umzumbe
N2
Southport
Marburg
Sea Park
Umtentweni
Port Shepstone
R61
Shelly Beach
Uvongo
Margate
INDIAN OCEAN

A
B
Free State
N3
R722
Bushman Paintings
Blockhouse
Harrismith
Phomolong
N5
Wilgerpark
Arcadia
Kidstone's Memorial 1931
De Beers Pass
Swinburne
Van Reenen
Hamilton
Klippoort
Lucitania
Hambrook
Ngula
Besters
Wyford
Van Reenen's Pass
Tugela
R103
Windsor Dam
Ladysmith
1
Sterkfontein Dam
Kerkenberg
Sterkfontein Dam Nature Reserve
Retief Rock
Diepkloof Dam
Geluksburg
Venter
Battle of Spioenkop 1899
Olivieshoek Pass
Wagon Hill
Metsimatsho Dam
R74
R616
Spioenkop Dam
Roosboom
Spioenkop Dam Nature Reserve
Woodstock Dam
Blockhouse
Bergville
MIDLANDS TOLL ROUTE
R600
Royal Natal National Park (World Heritage Site)
Driel Barrage
Winterton
N3
Source of the Orange River
Nxwaye
Zunckels
R74
Little Tugela
Frere
2
Loskop
Khubelu
Cathedral Peak
R600
DRAKENSBERG
Ndedema Gorge
Battle
Ntabamhlope
Sengu (Orange)
Moremoholo
Mafadi
Rockmount
Bushmans
Mafadi
3450m
Lammergeyer Hide
LESOTHO
A1
Mokhotlong
Giant's Castle
Klein-Mooi
3312
Natal Drakensberg Park
Redcliffe
Bobatsi
Mokhotlong
Sakeng
Redi
Loteni
A3
3
Linakaneng
Nhlathimbe
Highest point in Southern Africa
Thabana Ntlenyana
3842m
Linaheng
Mqatsheni
Lower Loteni
Sani Pass
Sani Pass
Mashai
Stepmore
Pholela
Netherby
97
Boesmansnek

C
D
104
Battle of Talana 1899
Malonjeni
Blood River
Battle of Blood River 1838
R68
Fort Mistake
Glencoe
Dundee
Sibongile
N11
R602
Nqutu
Biggarsberg
Vant's Drift
Battle of Rorke's Drift 1879
Totololo
Wasbank
Craigsforth
Battle of Elandslaagte 1899
Elandslaagte
Etholeni
Rorke's Drift
Battle of Isandlwana 1879
Helpmekaar
Elandskraal
Pepworth
Ekuvukeni
Amakhasi
Klipriver
Mahlaba
Doornkraal
Sundays
Pomeroy
Gordon Memorial
R33
KwaZulu-Natal
Battle of Colenso 1899
Mbango
Tugela Ferry
Tugela
Colenso
Bloukrans
Manyiseni
102
Chieveley
Weenen
Keate's Drift
Bloukrans Monument
Ehlanzeni
Mooi
Weenen Nature Reserve
Loza
Allandale
Estcourt
Muden
R74
Kranskloof
Saailaager
Greytown
Wagendrift Nature Reserve
Craigie Burn Nature Reserve
Nagendrift Dam
Craigie Burn Dam
General Louis Botha's Birthplace 1862
R103
R622
South Downs
Mooi River
Rietvlei
Umvoti Vlei
Sevenoaks
Karkloof Nature Reserve
R33
Rosetta
New Hanover
Dalton
Karkloof
York
Nottingham Road
N3
Albert Falls Dam
Albert Falls Nature Reserve
Mpolweni
Balgowan
R103
Fort Nottingham
Lidgetton
Howick
Albert Falls
R614
Wartburg
Umgeni
Merrivale
Midmar Dam
Queen Elizabeth Park
Colenso Mission Station 1854
Umgeni
Nagle Dam
Dargle
Midmar Public Resort and Nature Reserve
Hilton
Impendle
Gomane
Edendale
PIETERMARITZBURG
Boston
R617
98
Ashburton
Elandskop

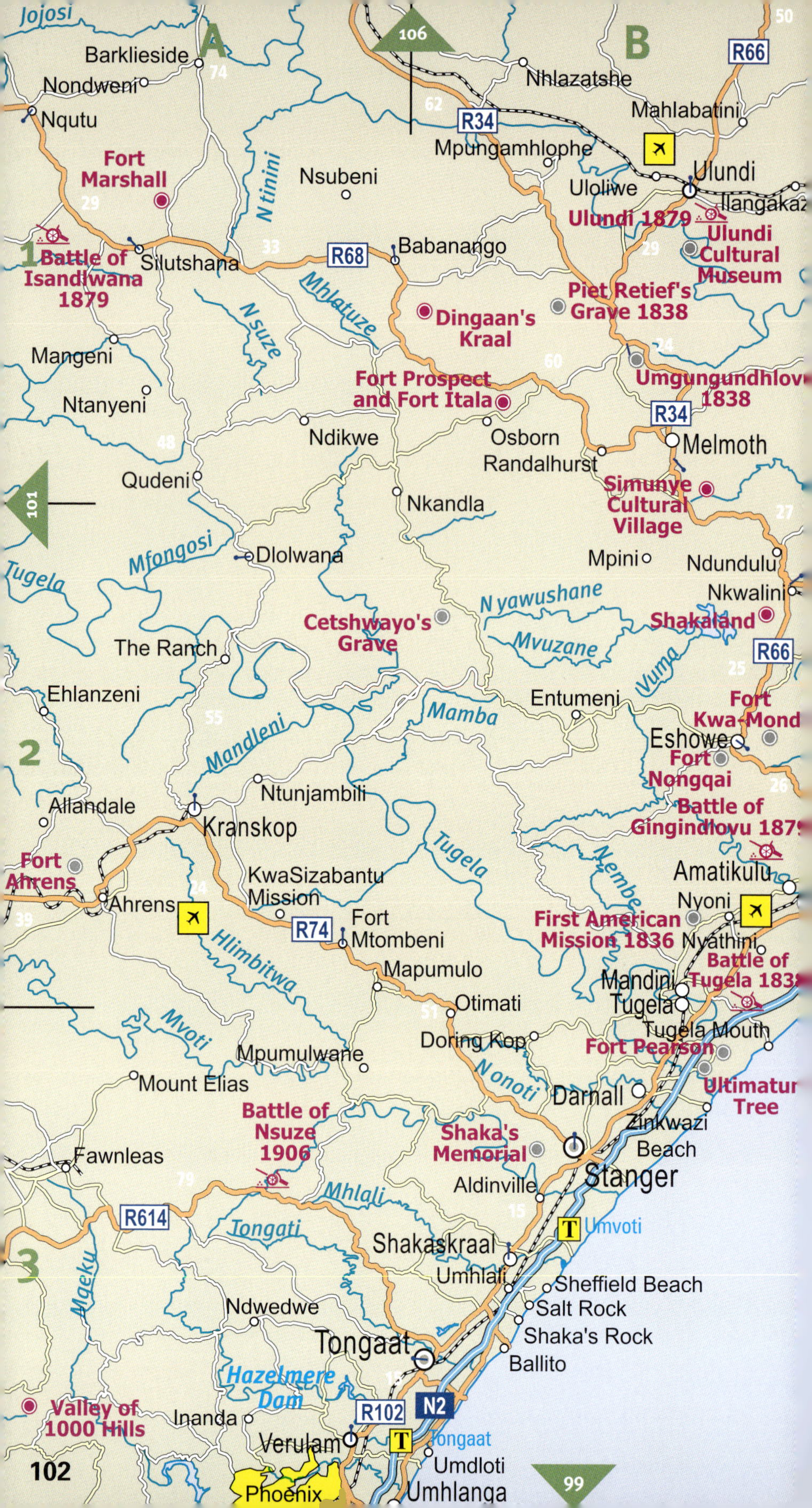

Jojosi
A
B
106
50
R66
Barklieside
74
Nondweni
Nqutu
Nhlazatshe
Mahlabatini
62
R34
Mpungamhlophe
Ulundi
Fort
Marshall
Nsubeni
Ntinini
Uloliwe
Ilangakazi
29
Ulundi 1879
Ulundi
Cultural
Museum
1
Battle of
Isandlwana
1879
Silutshana
33
R68
Babanango
29
Mhlatuze
Nsuze
Dingaan's
Kraal
Piet Retief's
Grave 1838
Mangeni
24
60
Fort Prospect
and Fort Itala
Umgungundhlovu
1838
Ntanyeni
R34
Ndikwe
Osborn
Melmoth
48
Randalhurst
Qudeni
Simunye
Cultural
Village
101
Nkandla
27
Dlolwana
Mpini
Ndundulu
Mfongosi
Tugela
Nyawushane
Nkwalini
Cetshwayo's
Grave
Shakaland
Mvuzane
The Ranch
R66
Vuma
25
Ehlanzeni
Entumeni
Fort
Kwa-Mondi
Mamba
55
Eshowe
2
Mandleni
Fort
Nongqai
Ntunjambili
26
Allandale
Battle of
Gingindlovu 1879
Kranskop
Tugela
Fort
Ahrens
KwaSizabantu
Mission
Amatikulu
Nembe
Nyoni
Ahrens
24
39
Fort
First American
Mission 1836
R74
Mtombeni
Nyathini
Hlimbitwa
Battle of
Mapumulo
Tugela 1838
Mandini
Otimati
51
Tugela
Tugela Mouth
Mvoti
Doring Kop
Fort Pearson
Mpumulwane
Nonoti
Ultimatum
Mount Elias
Tree
Darnall
Battle of
Nsuze
Zinkwazi
Shaka's
Beach
1906
Memorial
Stanger
Fawnleas
79
Aldinville
Mhlali
15
R614
Umvoti
Tongati
Shakaskraal
3
Umhlali
Mgeku
Sheffield Beach
Ndwedwe
Salt Rock
Shaka's Rock
Tongaat
Ballito
Hazelmere
Dam
19
Valley of
1000 Hills
R102
N2
Inanda
Verulam
Tongaat
Umdloti
99
Phoenix
Umhlanga

C
D
Hlabisa
107
Muntulu
Bushlands
Hluhluwe Dam
R618
Nyalazi
Mpila
Nselweni
Nyalazi River
Mambeni
Hluhluwe-Umfolozi Game Reserve
Somkele
N2
R618
St Lucia
Ondini
Munywana
Mtubatuba
Umunywana
River View
Mvamanzi
Mapelane Nature Reserve
Lake Eteza Nature Reserve
Teza
Cape St Lucia
Dondotsha
Ntabambanana
Nseleni
Kwa-Mbonambi
Mfule
Mposa
R34
Enseleni Nature Reserve
Mzingazi
Site of Shaka's Kraal
Empangeni
R34
Richards Bay
Felixton
Coward's Bush Monument
Mhlatuzi Lagoon
Cubhu
Richards Bay Game Reserve
Esikhawini
Mtunzini
Umlalazi Nature Reserve
T
R102
Mtunzini
N2
Gingindlovu
Fort Crealock
INDIAN OCEAN

A
B
Panbult
Vaal
Klein-Vaal
R35
R540
Witbank
Riet
Amersfoort
Mpumalanga
1
Heyshope Dam
R543
N11
Wiel
Assegaai
Perdekop
Latemanek
Dirkiesdorp
R23
Sand
Uitvlugt
Volksrust
Wakkerstroom
Pongola Bush Nature Reserve
Charlestown
Majuba 1881
Convention Bridge
Groenvlei
O'Neill's Cottage
Gansvlei
Laingsnek
BALELESBERG
Klipspruit
2
Ingogo
Dorp
Botha's Pass
Knight's Pass
R34
Skuinshoogte 1881
Utrecht
Seekoeivlei Nature Reserve
Kromellenboog
PL Uys Memoria
Madadeni
Free State
Newcastle
R34
Lennoxton
Osizweni
Muller's Pass
Ncandu Nature Reserve
Horn
Ballengeich
Rutland
Alcockspruit
Flint
Normandien Pass
R33
Glendale
Normandien
Dannhauser
Chelmsford Nature Reserve
Dejagersdrif
Horseshoe
R540
Ntshingwayo Dam
Hattingspruit
Dumaco
Talana Museum
3
Klippoort
R68
Battle of Talana 1899
Malonjeni
Fort Mistake
Glencoe
Dundee
Lucitania
R68
Sibongile
R602
Biggarsberg
Vant's Dr
R33
Craigsforth
Wasbank
N11
Totololo
101

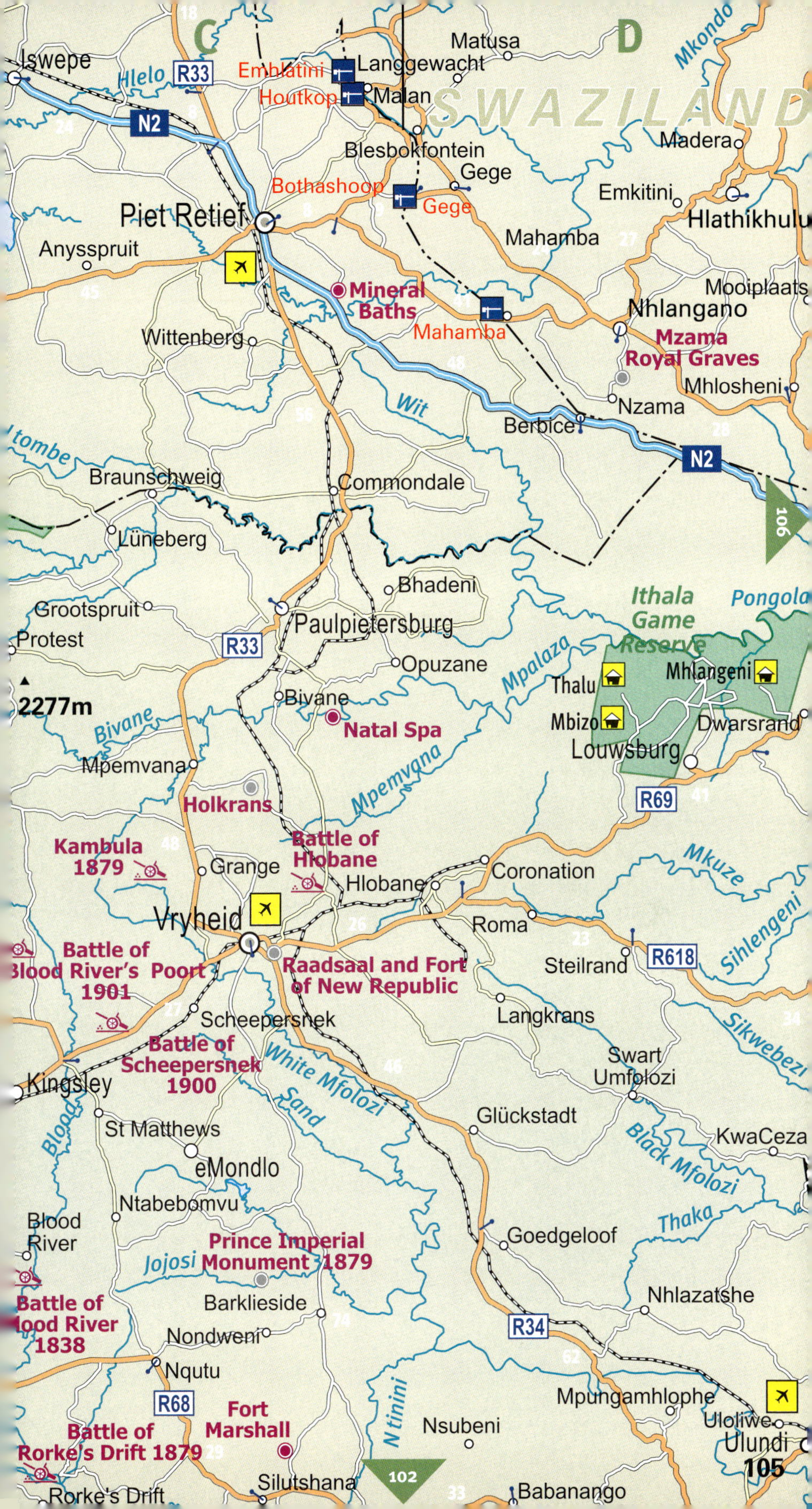
C
D
SWAZILAND
Iswepe
Hlelo
R33
N2
Emblatini
Houtkop
Langgewacht
Matusa
Malan
Blesbokfontein
Gege
Bothashoop
Gege
Madera
Emkitini
Hlathikhulu
Piet Retief
Anysspruit
Mahamba
Mineral Baths
Mahamba
Mooiplaats
Nhlangano
Mzama Royal Graves
Wittenberg
Mhlosheni
Nzama
Wit
Berbice
N2
Itombe
Braunschweig
Commondale
Lüneberg
106
Bhadeni
Grootspruit
Paulpietersburg
Protest
R33
Ithala Game Reserve
Pongola
Mpalaza
Opuzane
Thalu
Mhlangeni
2277m
Bivane
Natal Spa
Mbizo
Dwarsrand
Bivane
Louwsburg
Mpemvana
Mpemvana
R69
Holkrans
Kambula 1879
Battle of Hlobane
Mkuze
Grange
Hlobane
Coronation
Vryheid
Roma
Sihlengeni
Battle of Blood River's Poort 1901
Raadsaal and Fort of New Republic
Steilrand
R618
Scheepersnek
Langkrans
Battle of Scheepersnek 1900
Sikwebezi
Swart Umfolozi
Kingsley
White Mfolozi
Blood
Sand
St Matthews
Glückstadt
KwaCeza
Black Mfolozi
eMondlo
Ntabebomvu
Thaka
Blood River
Goedgeloof
Prince Imperial Monument 1879
Jojosi
Barklieside
Nhlazatshe
Battle of Blood River 1838
R34
Nondweni
Nqutu
Mpungamhlophe
R68
Fort Marshall
Ntinini
Uloliwe
Nsubeni
Ulundi
Battle of Rorke's Drift 1879
102
Silutshana
Rorke's Drift
Babanango

A
B
Van Eck Dam
Big Bend
Lulani
Kubutsa
Sithobela
Madera
Wisselrode
Mkondo
Mhlatuze
Emkitini
Hlathikhulu
Maloma
Lubuli
Nzila
Nsoko
LEBOMBO
1
Mooiplaats
SWAZILAND
Nhlangano
Memeze
Lismore
Mzama Royal Graves
Mlokolma Royal Graves
Excelsior
Ingwavuma
Mhlosheni
Paradys
Ndabazezwe
Nzama
Berbice
Hluthi
Sitilo
105
Onverwacht
Golela
Lavumisa
N2
Onverwacht
Golela
Jozini Dam
Zitende
Pongola
Casa Mia
Kingholm
Pongola
Pongola Poort Nature Reserve
Thalu
Ithala Game Reserve
Candover
R66
Mhlangeni
Dwarsrand
Magudu
R69
Mbizo
2
Louwsburg
Nkonkoni
R69
Mkuze
Mahlangasi
Mkuze
Sihlengeni
Mkuze Falls
N kunzana
R66
Steilrand
Ngome
Thokazi
R618
Royal Kraal
Zihlakenpele
Bululwana
Vuna
Sikwebezi
Swart Umfolozi
Nongoma
R618
Black Mfolozi
KwaCeza
R66
Thaka
Sigubudu
Mona
Bayeni
3
Muntulu
Nhlazatshe
Hlabisa
R618
Mahlabatini
Mpila
Nselweni
Mpungamhlophe
Ilangakazi
R34
Uloliwe
Ulundi
Mambeni
Ulundi 1879
Ulundi Cultural Museum
102
Hluhluwe-Umfolozi Game Reserve

C
D
MOZAMBIQUE
Nkonjane
Lusutfu
Catuane
Manhoca
Ponta do Ouro
Manhoca
Muzi
Ndumo Game Reserve
Tembe Elephant Reserve
Kosi Bay Nature Reserve
Ponta do Ouro
Ndumo
Mloli
Emanguzi
Boteler Point
Ku-Hlange Lake (Lake Kosi)
Pelindaba
Shemula
Maputaland
Pongola
Mseleni
Hully Point
Ndabeni
Lake Sibaya
Jozini
Tshongwe
Mbazwana
Jesser Point
Ubombo
Nhlonhlela
Emantuma
Sodwana Bay National Park
Lake Bhangazi
Mkuzi Game Reserve
Nhlohlela
UBOMBO
Msunduzi
Greater St Lucia Wetland Park (World Heritage Site)
Phinda Resource Reserve
INDIAN OCEAN
Bayala
Mhlosinga
Mkuze
Leven Point
Ngweni
Sodwana Bay National Park
Bird Island
N2
Memorial Gate
Lake St Lucia
Hluhluwe
Ncemane
Sodwana Bay National Park
Hluhluwe Dam
Cape Vidal
Bushlands
Bhangazi
Nyalazi
St Lucia Marine Reserve
Nyalazi River
Somkele
St Lucia
103

Index

NAME	GRID	PG	NAME	GRID	PG	NAME	GRID	PG	NAME	GRID	PG
Adam's Mission	C1	99	Gege	D1	105	Mbango	C2	101	Redcliffe	B3	100
Ahrens	A2	102	Geluksburg	B1	100	Mbazwana	D2	107	Redoubt	B3	98
Albert Falls	D3	101	Gingindlovu	C2	103	Melmoth	B1	102	Richards Bay	D2	103
Alcockspruit	A3	104	Glen Echo	C2	99	Memeze	A1	106	Richmond	B1	98
Aldinville	B3	102	Glencoe	A3	104	Merrivale	C3	101	Rietvlei	D3	101
Allandale	D2	101	Glendale	A3	104	Mhlosheni	A1	106	River View	D1	103
Amakhasi	C1	101	Glenmore Beach	B3	98	Mhlosinga	C3	107	Rockmount	B2	100
Amanzimtoti	D2	99	Glückstadt	D3	105	Mid-Illovo	C1	99	Rode	C3	97
Amatikulu	B2	102	Goba	B2	98	Mjika	A3	98	Roma	D2	105
Amersfoort	A1	104	Goedgeloof	D3	105	Mkuze	B2	106	Roosboom	B1	100
Anysspruit	C1	105	Golela	B2	106	Mloli	D1	107	Rorke's Drift	D1	101
Arcadia	A1	100	Gomane	C3	101	Mokhotlong	A3	100	Rosebank	C1	99
Ashburton	C1	99	Grange	C2	105	Mooi River	C2	101	Rosetta	C3	101
Babanango	A1	102	Greytown	D2	101	Mooiplaats	A1	106	Royal Kraal	B2	106
Balgowan	C3	101	Groenvlei	B2	104	Mount Ayliff	D3	97	Rustfontein	D2	97
Ballengeich	A3	104	Grootspruit	C2	105	Mount Elias	A3	102	Rutland	B3	104
Ballito	B3	102	Hambrook	B1	100	Mount Frere	C3	97	Salt Rock	B3	102
Banners Rest	B3	98	Hamilton	B1	100	Mountain View	A1	98	Scheepersnek	C3	105
Barklieside	C3	105	Hammarsdale	C1	99	Mpemvana	C2	105	Scottburgh	C2	99
Bayala	C2	107	Harding	A2	98	Mpini	B2	102	Sea Park	C3	99
Bayeni	A3	106	Harrismith	A1	100	Mpolweni	D3	101	Sehlabathebe	C1	97
Bazley	C2	99	Hattingspruit	B3	104	Mposa	D1	103	Sehonghong	C1	97
Beginsel	C2	97	Helpmekaar	D1	101	Mpumalanga	C1	99	Sevenoaks	D3	101
Berbice	A1	106	Hibberdene	C2	99	Mpumulwane	A3	102	Sezela	C2	99
Berbice	D1	105	Highflats	B2	98	Mpungamhlophe	B1	102	Shaka's Rock	B3	102
Bergville	A2	100	Hilton	C3	101	Mseleni	D2	107	Shakaskraal	A3	102
Besters	B1	100	Himeville	A1	98	Mtamvuna	A3	98	Sheffield Beach	B3	102
Bhadeni	C2	105	Hlabisa	B3	106	Mtubatuba	D1	103	Shelly Beach	C3	99
Big Bend	B1	106	Hlathikhulu	A1	106	Mtunzini	C2	103	Shemula	C1	107
Biggarsberg	A3	104	Hlobane	C2	105	Mtwalume	C2	99	Sibongile	B3	104
Bisi	A2	98	Hluhluwe	C3	107	Muden	D2	101	Sigubudu	B3	106
Bivane	C2	105	Hluthi	A1	106	Munster	B3	98	Silutshana	A1	102
Bizana	A3	98	Horseshoe	A3	104	Ncemane	C3	107	Sithobela	A1	106
Blesbokfontein	C1	105	Howick	C3	101	Ndabazezwe	B1	106	Sneezewood	A2	98
Blood River	C3	105	Ifafa	C2	99	Ndabeni	C2	107	Somkele	C1	103
Bomela	B3	98	Ifafa Beach	C2	99	Ndikwe	A1	102	South Downs	C2	101
Bontrand	A2	98	Ilangakazi	A3	106	Ndumo	C1	107	Southbroom	B3	98
Boston	B1	98	Impendle	C3	101	Ndundulu	B2	102	Southport	C3	99
Braemar	C2	99	Inanda	D1	99	Ndwedwe	A3	102	St Bernards	A2	98
Braunschweig	C1	105	Ingogo	A2	104	Netherby	A1	98	St Faith's	B2	98
Brooks Nek	D3	97	Ingwavuma	B1	106	New Amalfi	D2	97	St Joseph's	C2	99
Bulwer	A1	98	Iswepe	C1	105	New Hanover	D3	101	St Lucia	D1	103
Bushlands	C3	107	Ixopo	B2	98	Newcastle	A2	104	St Matthews	C3	105
Camperdown	C1	99	Izingolweni	B3	98	Ngabeni	A3	98	Stafford's Post	A2	98
Candover	B2	106	Jozini	C2	107	Ngome	A2	106	Stanger	B3	102
Casa Mia	B2	106	Keate's Drift	D2	101	Ngula	B1	100	Steilrand	D3	105
Catuane	C1	107	Kelso	C2	99	Ngweni	C3	107	Stepmore	B3	100
Cedarville	C2	97	Kingholm	B2	106	Nhlangano	D1	105	Swart Umfolozi	A2	102
Charlestown	A2	104	Kingsburgh	D2	99	Nhlazatshe	D3	105	Swartberg	D2	97
Chieveley	C2	101	Kingscote	D1	97	Nkandla	A1	102	Swinburne	A1	100
Clansthal	C2	99	Kingsley	C3	105	Nkonjane	C1	107	Tabankulu	D3	97
Clermont	D1	99	Klippoort	A3	104	Nkonkoni	B2	106	Teza	D1	103
Coleford	A1	98	Klipriver	C1	101	Nkwalini	B2	102	The Ranch	A2	102
Commondale	C1	105	Klipspruit	B2	104	Nondweni	C3	105	Thokazi	A2	106
Coronation	D2	105	Kokstad	D2	97	Nongoma	A3	106	Thornville	C1	99
Craigsforth	C1	101	Kranskloof	D2	101	Normandien	A3	104	Tina Bridge	C3	97
Creighton	A1	98	Kranskop	A2	102	Nottingham Road	C3	101	Tongaat	A3	102
Dalton	D3	101	Kromellenboog	A2	104	Nqabeni	B3	98	Tshongwe	C2	107
Dannhauser	B3	104	Kubutsa	A1	106	Nqutu	C3	105	Tsoelike	C1	97
Dargle	C3	101	KwaCeza	A3	106	Nsoko	B1	106	Tugela	B2	102
Darnall	B3	102	KwaDweshula	B2	98	Nsubeni	A1	102	Tugela Ferry	D2	101
Dejagersdrif	B3	104	KwaMashu	C1	99	Ntabambanana	C1	103	Tugela Mouth	B3	102
Dirkiesdorp	B1	104	Kwa-Mbonambi	D1	103	Ntabamhlope	B2	100	Turton	C2	99
Dlolwana	A2	102	KwaSizabantu			Ntabebomvu	C3	105	Ubombo	C2	107
Dondotsha	C1	103	Mission	A2	102	Ntanyeni	A1	102	Uitvlugt	B2	104
Donnybrook	A1	98	Langgewacht	C1	105	Ntunjambili	A2	102	Uloliwe	B1	102
Doornkraal	C1	101	Langkrans	D3	105	Nyalazi River	C3	107	Ulundi	C3	105
Doring Kop	B3	102	Latemanek	A1	104	Nyathini	B2	102	Umbumbulu	C1	99
Dorset	A2	98	Lavumisa	B1	106	Nyoni	B2	102	Umdloti	D1	99
Driefontein	C2	97	Lehlohonolo	C2	97	Nzama	D1	105	Umgababa	D2	99
Dududu	C2	99	Leisure Bay	B3	98	Nzila	A1	106	Umhlali	B3	102
Dumaco	A3	104	Lennoxton	A2	104	Oetting	B2	98	Umhlanga	D1	99
Dundee	B3	104	Lidgetton	C3	101	Onverwacht	A2	106	Umkomaas	C2	99
Durban	D1	99	Lismore	B1	106	Opuzane	C2	105	Umlazi	C1	99
Dwarsrand	A2	106	Loskop	B2	100	Osborn	B1	102	Umtentweni	C3	99
Eastwolds	B1	98	Louwsburg	A2	106	Osizweni	B3	104	Umunywana	C1	103
Edendale	C3	101	Lower Loteni	B3	100	Otimati	B2	102	Umzimkulu	A2	98
Ehlanzeni	A2	102	Lubuli	B1	106	Paddock	B3	98	Umzinto	C2	99
Ekuvukeni	C1	104	Lucitania	A3	104	Palm Beach	B3	98	Umzumbe	C3	99
Elandskop	B1	98	Lulani	B1	106	Panbult	B1	104	Underberg	A1	98
Elandskraal	D1	101	Lüneburg	C2	105	Paradys	A1	106	Utrecht	B2	104
Elandslaagte	C1	101	Madadeni	B3	104	Park Rynie	C2	99	Uvongo	C3	99
Emanguzi	D1	107	Madera	D1	105	Paulpietersburg	C2	105	Van Reenen	B1	100
Emkitini	D1	105	Mafube	C2	97	Pennington	C2	99	Vant's Drift	D1	101
eMondlo	C3	105	Mafusini	C3	97	Pepworth	C1	101	Verulam	D1	99
Empangeni	C2	103	Magudu	A2	106	Perdekop	A1	104	Volksrust	A2	104
Entumeni	B2	102	Magusheni	A3	98	Pevensey	A1	98	Vryheid	C2	105
Eshowe	B2	102	Mahamba	D1	105	Phoenix	B1	99	Wakkerstroom	B2	104
Esikhawini	C2	103	Mahlabatini	A3	106	Phomolong	A1	100	Wartburg	D3	101
Estcourt	C2	101	Mahlangasi	C1	105	Piet Retief	C1	105	Wasbank	C1	101
Etholeni	C1	101	Malan	B3	104	Pietermaritzburg	C1	99	Weenen	C2	101
Excelsior	B1	106	Maloma	A1	106	Pinetown	C1	99	Weza	A2	98
Fawnleas	A1	100	Malonjeni	B3	104	Pomeroy	D1	101	Wilgerpark	A1	100
Felixton	C2	103	Mandini	B2	102	Pongola	B2	106	Winterton	B2	100
Flagstaff	D3	97	Mangeni	A1	102	Ponta do Ouro	D1	107	Wisselrode	B1	100
Flint	B3	104	Manhoca	D1	107	Port Edward	B3	98	Wittenberg	C3	101
Fort Donald	A3	98	Manyiseni	D2	107	Port Shepstone	C3	99	Wyford	B1	100
Fort Mistake	A3	104	Mapumulo	A2	102	Protest	C2	105	York	B1	100
Fort Mtombeni	A3	102	Marburg	C3	99	Qacha's Nek	C2	97	Zihlakezide	B3	100
Franklin	D2	97	Margate	C3	99	Qudeni	A1	102	Zinkwazi Beach	B3	102
Frere	B2	100	Matatiele	C3	99	Queensburgh	C1	99	Zitende	A2	106
Friedenau	C2	99				Ramsgate	B3	98	Zunckels	B2	100
Gangala	B3	98	Matusi	D1	105	Randalhurst	B1	102			

Resources

KWAZULU-NATAL CONTACT DETAILS & INFORMATION

The following telephone numbers (and cyber connections) are as correct as possible at time of going to print. Numbers and codes do change over time, as do the names of establishments. For any queries dial 1023 (directory enquiries), 10118 (talking yellow pages) or visit www.yellowpages.co.za (electronic yellow pages).
NOTE: numbers listed are all phone numbers.

DURBAN CITY

Durban Exhibition Centre 031 301 7763

International Convention Centre Durban (ICC)
031 360 1000, www.icc.co.za

Durban Botanic Gardens
031 309 1170, www.durban.gov.za/parks

uShaka Marine World
031 368 6675, www.ushakamarineworld.co.za

SHOPPING CENTRES AROUND DURBAN

Heritage Market (Olde Main Road)
9 Olde Main Rd, Hillcrest, 031 765 2500

Kloof Village Mall (Olde Main Road)
33 Village Rd, Kloof, 031 764 5112

The Pavillion (Olde Main Road)
Spine Rd, Westville, 031 265 0558

Westville Mall (Olde Main Road)
3 Kensington Drive, Westville, 031 266 6382

Gateway Theatre of Shopping
(Northern Navigator)
031 566 2332, www.gatewayworld.co.za

La Lucia Mall (Northern Navigator)
031 562 8530, 031 562 8420

Windermere Centre (Morningside Meander)
163 Windermere Rd, 031 312 5959

The Wheel (uShaka Stretch)
55 Gillespie Str, South Beach
031 332 4324

Musgrave Centre (Musgrave Mile)
115 Musgrave Rd, 031 201 5129

The Workshop (The Bayside Beat)
031 304 9894

Wilson's Wharf Waterfront
031 307 7841, www.wilsonswharf.co.za

DURBAN AND SURROUNDS

Umgeni River Bird Park
031 579 4600, www.umgeniriverbirdpark.co.za

Beachwood Mangroves Swamps
031 274 1150, 082 559 2839

KZN Wildlife Office (Pietermaritzburg)
033 845 1000 / 1999
bookings@kznwildlife.com
www.kznwildlife.com
www.rhino.org.za

Inanda Heritage Route (Ethnic Tours)
031 902 1250 / 4178, 072 245 3339
www.ethnictours.co.za
ethnictours@medi.co.za

Kenneth Stainbank Nature Reserve
031 469 2807, 083 423 0843

Krantzkloof Nature Reserve
031 764 3515

Bluff Nature Reserve
031 469 2807, 083 423 0843

Pinetown Tourism Office
Info 031 777 1874

The Monastery Tea Garden
(Mariannhill Monastery)
031 700 2706, 083 635 7526

Pinetown Japanese Tea Garden
031 701 8821

Sugar Coast Tourism
031 561 4257, www.sugarcoast.kzn.org.za

Resources

THE NORTH COAST

Umhlanga (Sugar Coast Tourism)
031 561 4257

Umhlanga Lagoon Nature Reserve
 031 561 1682, 031 566 4018

The Dolphin Coast Publicity Association
(Ballito, Shaka's Rock, Salt Rock)
032 946 1997 / 2434
www.dolphincoast.kzn.org.za
info@thedolphincoast.co.za

Gingindlovu (Eshowe Tourism Office)
035 337 1217, 035 474 1141

Mtunzini Tourism
035 474 1141 ext 259

Umlalazi Municipality
035 474 1141, www.umlalazi.org.za

Umlalazi Nature Reserve
035 340 1836 / 9

Eshowe Tourism & Publicity
035 474 1141, 474 2348 (Fort Nonqai)

ZULULAND

Richards Bay & Empangeni
(uMhlathuze Tourism Office) 035 753 3909

Enseleni Nature Reserve (Richards Bay)
035 753 2212

Ulundi Tourism
035 870 0034, 083 766 5942

Zululand Tourism (Ulundi)
Info 035 870 0812

Ulundi KZN Wildlife Office
035 870 0552

Melmoth Information Centre
035 450 7572

Simunye Zulu Lodge
035 450 3111
www.proteahotels.com/simunye

Shakaland
035 460 0912, www.shakaland.com
res@shakaland.com

Lake Sibaya
Sibaya lake lodge
011 616 8232
www.lake-sibaya.co.za

Cape Vidal National Park
035 590 9012

ZULULAND PARKS & RESERVES

The Greater St Lucia Wetland Park
(St Lucia Wetland Reserve)
KZN Wildlife 033 845 1000
www.kznwildlife.com

Greater St Lucia Wetland Park Authority
035 590 1528

St Lucia Information Centre
035 590 1247 / 1047
www.stlucia.co.za

St Lucia Tourism Bureau
035 590 1075

St Lucia KZN Wildlife Office
035 590 1340 / 341

Matubatuba Municipality (St Lucia)
035 590 1339

Sodwana Bay
035 571 0051 / 2 / 3
sodwana@kznwildlife.com

Kosi Bay
035 592 0234

Turtle hotline
035 590 1162 (leather back turtles)

Mozambique
Maputo Elephant Reserve / Inhaca Island
Mozambique Tourism
09 258 142 6623

Resources

THE SOUTH COAST

Amanzimtoti Publicity Association
031 903 7498 / 3
www.amanzimtoti.org.za
info@amanzimtoti.org.za

Amanzimtoti Bird Sanctuary
031 913 4572, 082 741 3094

Kingsburgh (Amanzimtoti Info Office)
031 903 7498 / 3

TC Robertson Nature Reserve
Scottburgh (Umdoni coast & Country Tourism)
039 976 1364

Vernon Crookes Nature Reserve
039 974 2222, 083 293 3622

Hibberdene Hibiscus Coast Tourism Office
039 699 3203 / 2020
hibberdene@hibiscuscoast.org.za

Hibberdene
Mzimayi River Lodge and Restaurant
039 699 3307

Port Shepstone (Hibiscus Coast Tourism Office)
039 682 2455
portshepstone@hibiscuscoast.org.za

Oribi Gorge Nature Reserve
039 679 1644, 083 284 9326

Banana Express
039 682 4821, 072 112 1136
www.banana-express.co.za
acrailmc@venturenet.co.za

Margate Hibiscus Coast Tourism Office
039 312 2322 / 3 / 4
margate@hibiscuscoast.org.za

Uvongo (Hibiscus Coast Tourism)
039 317 4630
Shelley Beach Tourism 039 315 5168 / 1886
Margate Tourism 039 312 2322

Hibiscus Coast Tourism Head Office
039 317 4630
www.hibiscuscoast.kzn.org.za
admin@hibiscuscoast.org.za

Uvongo River Nature Reserve
039 315 7378

Ramsgate (Hibiscus Coast Tourism)
039 317 4630

Umtamvuna Nature Reserve
039 311 2383

Port Edward
039 313 1211
portedward@hibiscuscoast.org.za

Southern Explorer (South Coast Info)
083 446 2348
www.southernexplorer.co.za
info@southernexplorer.co.za

Kokstad
039 747 9077

East Griqualand Outdoors
(EG Outdoors For Information On Kokstad)
039 747 9077
www.eastgriqualand.kzn.org.za

Explore East Griqualand
039 727 4444
www.exploreeg.com
exploreeg@futurenet.co.za

Mount Currie Nature Reserve
039 727 3844

Route 617
Sani Saunter (Southern Drakensberg)
033 702 1902, 701 1471
info@sanisaunter.com

Ixopo Tourism
083 270 0403

KLOOF TO PIETERMARITZBURG

Valley Of 1000 Hills Tourism
031 777 1874, www.1000hills.kzn.org.za
info@tourism-1000hills.com

Pietermaritzburg Tourism
033 345 1348 / 9, 033 345 1451
www.pietermaritzburg.co.za
www.pmbtourism.co.za
www.pmb-midlands.kzn.org.za
info@pmbtourism.co.za
admin@pmbtourism.org.za

Howick Tourism Office
(Howick Midmar information)
033 330 5305, www.howick.org.za

Albert Falls Area
033 569 0010, 082 708 4246

Midlands Meander Tourism
033 330 8195
www.midlandsmeander.co.za
info@midlandsmeander.co.za

Mooi River Publicity Association
033 263 1833, 082 447 2082

Resources Resources Resources

BUSHMANS RIVER REGION

Bushmans River Tourism Association
036 352 6253, 083 556 2206
www.bushmans.co.za
brta@futurest.co.za
info@bushmans.co.za

Estcourt
Umtshezi Municipality 036 352 3000

Weenen Nature Reserve
036 354 7013

Spioenkop Dam Nature Reserve
036 488 1578

THE DRAKENSBERG

Winterton (Drakensberg Adventure)
036 488 1988, 488 1207

Bergville (Drakensberg Tourism)
036 448 1557 / 1296

Drakensberg Adventure Route
036 488 1988

The Drakensberg Tourism Association
036 448 1557, 448 1296, 448 1551

Lesotho Tourism Office
09 266 321 428
Northern Drakensberg

Central Drakensberg Information Centre
036 488 1207

Southern Drakensberg Sani Saunter
033 701 1471, 702 1902
info@sanisaunter.com
www.sanisaunter.com

BATTLEFIELDS

Battlefields Route
082 802 1643
www.battlefields.kzn.org.za
route@battlefields.org.za

Greytown Community Tourism Association
033 413 9124, 033 413 1171

Colenso Tourism Information
036 637 2992, 036 422 2111

Ladysmith Tourism
036 637 2992
www.ladysmith.co.za
info@ladysmith.co.za

Tourism Dundee
034 212 2121 ext 2262
www.tourdundee.co.za
tourism@dundeekzn.co.za

Tourism Newcastle
034 315 3318
www.tourismnewcastle.co.za
www.newcastle.co.za
info@newcastle.co.za

Chelmsford Game Reserve
034 351 1753 / 4 / 5, 072 122 5571

Chelmsford Game Reserve (Head Office)
033 845 1374

Utrecht Publicity Association
034 331 3613
utrechtmun@telkomsa.net

Utrecht Balele Community Game Park
034 331 3041 ext 206
utrechtmun@telkomsa.net

Vryheid Information Bureau
034 982 2133 ext 2229
www.vryheid.co.za
information@vhd.dorea.co.za

Vryheid Hill Nature Reserve
034 983 2098, 072 712 6713

Paulpietersburg Publicity Association
034 995 1650 ext 219
admin@pmbtourism.co.za

Ithala Game Reserve
034 983 2540, 033 845 1000